Heinemann **Scottish** History
for Standard Grade

S.A.T.H.

KU-307-339

Edith Girvan

Series editor: Jim McGonigle

Changing Life in Scotland and Britain: 1830s–1930s

www.heinemann.co.uk
✓ Free online support
✓ Useful weblinks
✓ 24 hour online ordering

01865 888058

Heinemann

Inspiring generations

Heinemann is an imprint of Pearson Education Limited,
a company incorporated in England and Wales, having
its registered office at Edinburgh Gate, Harlow, Essex, CM20 2JE.
Registered company number: 872828

Heinemann is a registered trademark of Pearson Education Limited

© Pearson Education Limited, 2004

First published 2004

10
10 9 8 7 6

British Library Cataloguing in Publication Data is available
from the British Library on request.

ISBN: 978 0 435326 92 0

Copyright notice
All rights reserved. No part of this publication may be reproduced in any form or by any means (including photocopying
or storing it in any medium by electronic means and whether or not transiently or incidentally to some other use of this
publication) without the written permission of the copyright owner, except in accordance with the provisions of the
Copyright, Designs and Patents Act 1988 or under the terms of a licence issued by the Copyright Licensing Agency, 90
Tottenham Court Road, London W1T 4LP. Applications for the copyright owner's written permission should be
addressed to the publisher.

Designed by Hicksdesign
Produced by Kamae Design, Oxford

Original illustrations © Pearson Education Limited, 2004

Illustrated by Kamae Design, John Storey

Printed in China (CTPS/06)

Photographic acknowledgements
The author and the publisher should like to thank the following for permission to
reproduce photographs:
Cover photo, Science & Society Picture Library; page 10, Universities of Glasgow and Edinburgh Archives; page 12,
Bridgeman Art Library/Robert Fleming Holdings; page 15, Mary Evans Picture Library; page 20, Hulton Archive; page
23, Mary Evans Picture Library; page 26, Mary Evans Picture Library; page 28, Bridgeman Art Library; page 29,
EpicScotland; page 30, Bridgeman Art Library; page 33, Martin Fogarty/Firuda National School, Co Kilkenny; page 34,
Mary Evans Picture Library; page 37, Hulton Archive; page 41, Hulton Archive; page 42, Bridgeman Art Library; page
45, Mary Evans Picture Library; page 47, Hulton Archive; page 48, Hulton Archive; page 53, Hulton Archive; page 52,
Hulton Archive; page 59, Bridgeman Art Library/British Museum; page 60 (left)/(right), Dundee Central Library; page
60, Hulton Archive; page 61, Hulton Archive; page 62, Glasgow City Archives; page 68, Mary Evans Picture Library;
page 70, Mary Evans Picture Library; page 75, Corbis; page 76, Bridgeman Art Library; page 77, Mary Evans Picture
Library; page 80, Bridgeman Art Library; page 81 (top), Bridgeman Art Library; page 81 (bottom), Hulton Archive; page
82, Museum of London; page 83, Mary Evans Picture Library; page 85, Hulton Archive.

Picture research by Beatrice Ray

Written source acknowledgements
The author and publisher gratefully acknowledge the following publications from which written sources in the book are drawn. In some sentences
the wording or sentence structure has been simplified:
5A,B S.L. Case, *Industrial Revolution* (Evans Bros, 1975)
11F R.K. Kelsall, *Population: The Social Structure of Britain* (Longman, 1967)
12G D. MacLeod, *Gloomy Memories in the Highlands of Scotland* (Thompson, 1857)
31H I. Carter, *Farmlife in Northeast Scotland 1840–1914: The Poor Man's Country* (Edinburgh, 1979)
36G A.S. Cunningham, *Mining in Mid and East Lothian: history of the industry from earliest times to the present day* (James Thin, 1925)
44E J. McDonald, *Life Jottings of an Old Edinburgh Citizen* (T.N. Foulis, 1915)
45F J. Francis, *A History of the English Railway: its social relations and revelations 1820–1845* (Longman, 1851)
46I I. Olson, *The Day the Railways came to Strichen* (Leopard, 1944)
49K J. Kerr, *Leaves from an Inspector's Logbook* (Thomas Nelson, 1915)
49L R.N. Rundle, *Britain's Economic and Social Development from 1700 to the Present Day* (Hodder Arnold, 1973)
51A G. Sims, *Living London* (Cassell & Co., 1902)
54D C. Dickens, *Sketches by Boz* (Chapman and Hall, 1839)
54F G. Sims, *Living London* (Cassell and Co., 1902)
55G W.C. Preston and A. Mearns, *The Bitter Cry of Outcast London* (James Clarke and Co., 1883)
56I G. McAllister, *Houses that are Homes* (Blackie, 1945)
58M G. Godwin and J. Brown, *Another Blow for Life* (W.H.Allen, 1864)
68A C. Dickens, *The Pickwick Papers* (Chapman and Hall, 1837)
76B A. Holdsworth, *Out of the Doll's House* (BBC, 1988)
77D A. Holdsworth, *Out of the Doll's House* (BBC, 1988)
Acknowledgements
Every effort has been made to contact copyright holders of material reproduced in this book. Any omissions will be
rectified in subsequent printings if notice is given to the publishers.

The publishers gratefully acknowledge the contribution of the late John Doogan to the writing of this book.

CONTENTS

INTRODUCTION
Changing life in Scotland and Britain: 1830s–1930s

What's it all about?

In this book you will learn about:
- changes in agriculture and industry
- changes in population: looking at migration from the Highlands and immigration from Ireland
- living in the countryside
- changes in industry: the coal mining industry
- changes in transport: the railway industry
- housing and health in towns
- the growth of democracy
- the changing role of women: their struggle for the vote and their role in the First World War

in the hundred years between the 1830s and the 1930s.

The period 1830 to 1930 is one of the most exciting in Scottish and British history. It was a period of change – dramatic change, which would mould the country to look the way it does today. This period was one of great movement of people, of invention, and of major changes to the way people worked and carried out their everyday lives. In the years 1831 to 1931, the population in Scotland increased from 2,364,000 to 4,842,980. This rising population did not remain static but moved to the fast-growing new industrial towns.

The reasons behind this increase and change involve factors that all impact on one another.

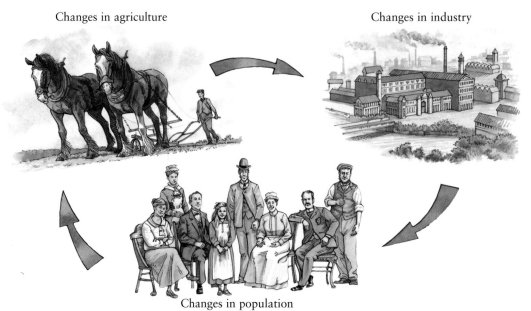

Changes in agriculture

Changes in industry

Changes in population

Glossary

agriculture: dealing with farming and the land.

industry: dealing with the production of goods, often in factories.

Sources A and B are from S. L. Case in his book *Industrial Revolution* (1975).

Source A

The rapid increase in population of this country in the eighteenth century meant that each year there were more mouths to feed. As a result, farming had to change to keep up with the demand for food. This change in farming methods is usually called the Agricultural Revolution.

Source B

During the eighteenth century, the population of Britain nearly doubled … as a result, there was a much bigger demand for British goods both at home and abroad … it was quite impossible to meet all these new demands while goods were still made by hand at people's own homes … the answer was provided by machines and factories. This important change from hand work in the home to machine work in factories is usually known as the Industrial Revolution.

⋯ Activity

In groups of three or four, choose any one of the topics mentioned in the 'What's it all about?' box opposite.

Using the Internet, class or school library, find out what you can about the topic in 1830 and then in 1930.

Prepare a wall display to show the situation in 1830, then in 1930. Identify the changes that have taken place within this topic during the hundred years that have elapsed. Using your display, report your findings back to the rest of the class.

WRITING GUIDANCE

In the Standard Grade exam, the extended writing task will be worth eight marks and it can appear in any unit of the paper: I, II or III. In this question you will be given marks for structure. If you stick to the following rules, you will succeed at this type of question.

- You must begin with a brief introduction.
- You should then write three or four paragraphs relevant to the question.
- You should reach a conclusion that clearly answers the question being asked.

EXAMPLE QUESTION

Explain why so many people left the Highlands in the nineteenth century.

ANSWER

Introduction

There were many reasons why people left the Highlands in the nineteenth century and one of the main ones concerned what became known as the Highland Clearances. However, there were other factors such as a blight on the potato crop, the hardships suffered by the Highlanders, the lack of jobs and the attraction of life overseas.

Paragraph 1

Many people left the land through the forceful action of their landlords. The landlords had come to realise that rearing sheep on the land was more profitable than allowing crofters to rent the land and, as a result, many people were forced to move to the Lowlands or overseas.

Paragraph 2

The growth in leisure pursuits for the rich also had an impact on the way land was used in the Highlands. Deer farming and hunting became very fashionable and the thought of profit also induced owners to force their tenants off the land.

Paragraph 3

As in Ireland, the Highlands fell victim to the potato blight. Most farmers grew a large amount of potatoes in the north of Scotland and when the blight struck the crops, starvation struck the people. Many people were forced off the land as a result.

Paragraph 4

Changes in other industries led to people moving. For example, machinery took away work from cottage industries, such as handloom weaving, and so many Highlanders had no back-up to help support their households. This pushed some people to a level at which they could not survive and so the attraction of factory work in the towns grew.

Paragraph 5

Not all people left, however, because of hardship: many left because of opportunities abroad. Higher wages and a warmer climate pulled people away from their home to a better life overseas.

Conclusion

In conclusion, it can be seen that while the Clearances had an impact on the movement of people away from the Highlands in the nineteenth century, so, too, did the potato famine and resultant starvation. With the increasing mechanisation of nineteenth-century industry, tenants forced off the land were not able to turn to cottage industries in order to supplement their income.

For some, the attraction of jobs and higher wages providing hope of a better standard of living, contributed to the exodus from the Highlands.

ANSWERING A KNOWLEDGE AND UNDERSTANDING QUESTION

There are three main types of Knowledge and Understanding question.

- ■ Describe an event or happening.

- ■ Explain why something has happened or the results of an event.

- ■ Explain the importance of an event.

To get full marks you need to include some recall information: in other words, a piece of information that is not in the source provided. The following question and answer demonstrates this. Recall information is highlighted.

Question

Source A was written by Chris Allen and describes Enclosures in Dolphinstoun.

Source A

> In addition to crops and livestock, close attention was given to what the new-style farmstead, suitable for the more prosperous, should comprise. By 1805, the average acreage of a mixed arable farm was 200 acres, significantly larger than the 60 acres of before.

1 Describe the changes brought about by Enclosures.

Answer

In the early nineteenth century, the land had been divided into narrow strips of land or runrigs. The Enclosures meant that the rigs were combined and enclosed with a hedge or wall to make larger fields. These were good for the wealthier farmers who could afford to buy the land. The size of farms grew from small holdings to much larger farms. Crops and livestock changed. The enclosed farms enabled farmers to rent their land for a longer period of time and so they were willing to try to improve farming. New improvements included proper drainage and a more scientific approach to farming.

Comment

This answer is well balanced, with knowledge and information taken from the source as well as recalled knowledge. In total, there are four points from the source and nine from recall. A marker would expect to see both demonstrated in an answer. Here, the answer shows clearly that the question has been answered properly and that the candidate has a clear knowledge of the topic in question. Background knowledge has helped lead into the answer and shows an organised approach to the question.

ANSWERING AN ENQUIRY SKILLS QUESTION

There are six main types of Enquiry question.

■ Evaluating a source.

■ Comparing sources.

■ Selecting evidence from sources.

■ Discussing the view of an author.

■ Evaluating how complete a source is.

■ Reaching a balanced conclusion using evidence from sources and recalled knowledge.

When evaluating the usefulness of a source it is always important to make sure that the marker cannot question something you have written by asking 'So what?' If you can answer this, you need to add it to your answer. To do this you must make sure that you have discovered:

■ when the source was produced

■ who produced the source

■ why the source was produced

■ what the source tells us

■ if the source is trustworthy.

Question

Source B was part of a report written in 1814 by Sir John Sinclair, a farmer and improver who was also an MP.

Source B

> The great advantage to Scotland of threshing mills being now so common is that the amount of manual labour is now greatly reduced. Also, the quantity of agricultural produce is greatly increased. Managing farming on large estates has become much easier.

1   How useful is Source B for finding out about changes in farming after 1800?

Answer

···> *When?* Source B was written in 1814 during the time of changes in farming.

···> *Who?* It was written by Sir John Sinclair, an improver and farmer in the 1800s. He was also a Member of Parliament.

···> *What does it say?* In his article, he points out the advantages of the new machines and the impact they have had on reducing manual labour.

···> *Can we trust it?* However, it should be noted that he is giving his opinion on the changes to farming and as an improver himself would be giving one point of view.

···> *Why?* As the purpose of the report would be to persuade other farmers to adopt new machines, it would only look at one standpoint and does not look at any of the drawbacks about the changes.

Comment

In this answer, the candidate has worked systematically through the rubric (the description of the source at the start) and then looked at the content of the source before reaching a conclusion as to whether the source was indeed useful for the topic in question.

CHANGES IN POPULATION

What was the impact of Britain's increasing population?

What's it all about?

The impact of the increasing population in Britain was huge. At this time, there was also a movement of people, both from the countryside into cities, and also between different parts of the country. In this chapter, you will learn some of the reasons why this happened.

INCREASE AND MOVEMENT IN BRITAIN'S POPULATION

There were many reasons for the increase in Britain's population.

- Improvements in farming meant that a better quality of food was being produced and people had a healthier diet.
- Improvements in medicine (for example, smallpox vaccination) meant that people lived longer, and children in particular survived into adulthood.
- People were marrying younger and having more children.
- During the second half of the nineteenth century, housing and water supplies had improved. Better hygiene helped prevent the spread of disease.
- Immigration was also a factor by the mid 1800s, with large numbers of people moving into the country from Ireland.

Glossary

census: an official count of the population carried out every ten years.

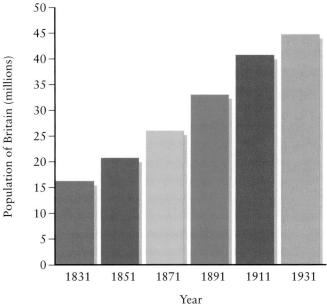

Population increase in Britain, 1831–1931.

Information on the population in the late 1700s is difficult to obtain as there was no official population count or **census** until 1801. Any figures on the population are to an extent guesses, although we do have evidence about the population from the Old Statistical Account of the 1790s. This was a collation of information about parishes in Scotland compiled by Sir John Sinclair. The information for each shire was then published in a huge volume.

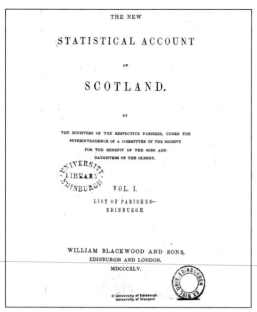

The front cover of a New Statistical Account of 1845.

The 1830s saw an updated version also based on the work of local ministers. It was known as the New Statistical Account.

> 1   Why would the Old Statistical Account be useful to someone trying to find out about the population of Scotland in the 1790s?
>
> 2   Can you think of any reasons why the Old Statistical Accounts might not be useful for finding out about the population in the 1790s?

Not only was the population increasing but where people lived was also changing. The new towns attracted many away from the countryside. The following sources are all from the New Statistical Accounts published in the 1830s.

Source A

Since 1811, the population in Newbattle has been gradually increasing and the only way to explain it is the extension to the mines of the Marquis of Lothian.

Newbattle, East Lothian, 1834.

Source B

The increase in population is owing to the coal works in the parish and the nearby iron works.

Airdrie, Lanarkshire, 1836.

Source C

The cause of the extraordinary increase in population is due to the great growth of the linen trade, which has produced many spinning mills ... By giving employment to thousands, it has encouraged early marriages, as well as bringing families from other parts of Scotland and from Ireland.

Dundee, 1837.

Source D

The increase in population may be explained by the ease with which even boys, employed at weaving, get possession of money; able to earn considerable wages, many hurry into matrimony.

Lesmahagow, Lanarkshire, 1836.

> 1   Using evidence from sources A to D, explain some of the reasons for population increase in these areas in the 1800s.
>
> 2   What additional information is included in Source F to explain this increase?

Source E

The town of Aberdeen is much enlarged. Many flock here from the country and the Highland parts in search of employment. Early marriage and large families is the common way of it now ... with children set to labour as young as five or six.

Aberdeen in the 1830s.

In Aberdeen, the population rose from 27,500 in 1801 to 153,500 in 1901.

Source F

Industrialisation brought about a revolution in social habits and customs. It was no longer necessary to wait until land became available before marrying and starting a family. A full wage could be earned in a factory or mine by the age of eighteen or so. People were free to marry younger and did so in large numbers. Marriages at an early age tended to produce more children and many more of these children survived into adulthood than ever before. The increase in births in the early nineteenth century easily outpaced the very high death rates.

Population: The Social Structure of Britain, R.K. Kelsall (1967).

THE HIGHLAND CLEARANCES

The 1800s was a period of turmoil in the Highlands of Scotland. Landowners and crofters came into conflict, resulting in a mass **exodus** of people from the north of Scotland to Lowland Scotland and as far away as America, Australia and New Zealand.

Crofting

The 1800s were a bad time for those who lived on the **crofts** of Scotland. The crofting system worked whereby in return for an annual rent landlords provided people with small plots of land – plots were kept deliberately small so that the occupants would have to take on extra work for the benefit of the landlord. However, landlords did not make a great deal of money from this method of working and soon became aware of other ways by which the land could yield more profits. Sheep farming, in particular using some of the new breeds of sheep, was one of the ways in which landlords could make money without the trouble involved in renting land to tenant farmers. With the arrival of the profitable sheep-farming industry, and later deer farming, many crofters were **evicted** from their homes: this was known as the Highland Clearances.

Glossary

exodus: moving away from a place, usually in large numbers.

crofts: smallholdings or farms.

evicted: thrown off their property.

kelp: brown seaweed.

TIMELINE

1790s	The Great Cheviot (breed of sheep) brought to Ross and Caithness.
1800	First Clearances in Sutherland.
1801	Beginning of evictions.
1807	Ninety families removed from their homes. The Northern Association of Gentlemen Farmers and Breeders of Sheep resolve to extend this practice to other parts of the Highlands.
1811–13	Sutherland Clearances.
1817	Sheep farming market established in Inverness.
1820s	Riots in Sutherland and Ross and the decline of the **kelp** industry.
1832	Outbreak of cholera.
1836–7	Famine.
1840s	More evictions throughout the Highlands.
1850s	Deer farming becomes popular and a decline in evictions starts.
1852	The Highland and Island Emigration Society formed, offering ships and assistance.
1886	Crofting Act makes it difficult to evict Highlanders.

In the years between the mid-1700s and the late 1800s, the population of the Highlands of Scotland fell dramatically. As roads improved during the early 1800s, new opportunities for trade with the textile mills to the south emerged. Sheep such as the Great Cheviot were brought into Scotland to provide wool. The crofters on the land were no longer needed. Some of the most infamous evictions took place in Sutherland.

In the guise of making farming improvements and gaining more from the land, it was planned to move all the tenants to the sea coast of the estate in order that the interior of the land could be devoted to making profits from wool and mutton for the ever-increasing English market.

In 1814, the evictions began in Strathnaver. Tenants were ordered out of their homes, which were burnt. If anyone was slow in getting their belongings from their homes or too slow in leaving their homes, the fire was started while they were still inside. A **clergyman** named Donald MacLeod, in his book *Gloomy Memories*, recorded the tragedies involved in much of what happened.

Areas of Scotland most affected by the Highland Clearances in the 1800s.

Areas most affected by the Highland Clearances.

Glossary

clergyman: a member of the clergy, minister, priest.

Source G

I saw the townships set on fire. Grummore with sixteen houses and Archmilidh with four. All the houses were burnt with the exception of one. A barn. Few if any of the families knew where to turn their heads or from whom to get their next meal. It was sad, the driving away of these people.

Roderick MacLeod, a witness to the evictions, quoted in *Gloomy Memories* (1857) by Donald MacLeod.

Highlanders were evicted from their homes in the 1800s as part of the Highland Clearances, as depicted here in Thomas Faed's 'The Last of the Clan' (1865).

Source H

Women had to put the children in carts beside their husbands, who were tied up and unable to assist them. Helpless men were tied up on the pier and then thrown like cargo into the hold of the ship. They all left for the streets of Glasgow or the frozen wastes of Canada. Many of them died of hunger or fever going across the ocean. Only God knows the evil work of that day.

An account by Catherine McPhee, written in the 1880s, describing what she saw in 1848.

Source I

Well, Janet, the Countess will never **flit** you again …

A 90-year-old man, who was burned out of his home and whose wife died as a result of the eviction, quoted at his wife's graveside in 1813.

There are countless other such horror stories of the way the Highlanders were treated at the time of the Clearances. Many starved and froze to death at the site where their homes had been. Some died of exposure, disease or fatigue. Starvation was everywhere.

Source J

Scotch people are of happier **constitution** and do not fatten like the larger breed of animals.

The Countess of Sutherland, unperturbed by the Clearances, in a letter to a friend in 1813.

Glossary

flit: move.

constitution: general health or well-being.

descendants: people who have come after their ancestors.

This attitude was common among the landlords and officials at the time. In Strathaird in Skye, when the landlord wanted to clear over 600 people off his land, the local sheriff went to inform the people.

Source K

He has a perfect right to turn you out of your dwellings and possessions and to call upon me and other authorities to aid him.

Local sheriff, Strathaird, Skye.

Source L

I have been increasing my sheep stock as the removal of crofters made space. The crofters could not pay their rents. The population, which was 500, is reduced to 150. Five of the families got crofts on other properties. Two of the crofters are in Tobermory; all the others went to America, Australia or the south of Scotland.

Estates owner, Francis Clark, 1851.

Even as recently as 1992, one of the **descendants** of the Countess of Sutherland continued to justify and defend the actions of his ancestors.

Source M

The people who lived on the estate … were really in the process of starving to death and were living in disgraceful conditions, conditions that no civilised person could have supported, and which certainly would not be tolerated for half a second today.

Lord Strathnaver, speaking on a television programme (1992).

The actions of the lairds or Scottish landlords were 'push' factors forcing the people to leave the land. As well as the lairds wanting to use their land for sheep, deer and hunting for the wealthy, nature provided another problem for the Highlanders in 1845, as it had done the previous year in Ireland – a blight on the potato crop.

Some landlords, however, were scared they might be asked to support the **evictees** and actively encouraged people to emigrate: this was a much cheaper option for them! On the island of Lewis, for example, 2000 people were persuaded to emigrate.

Glossary

evictees: people who have been thrown off their property.

Source N

Sir James has offered to provide 1000 free passages for people and their families as may desire to emigrate, to cancel all debts due to him and to leave them their stock. If anyone now in arrears of rent of two years and who has not the means till the next harvest should reject this offer without good reason, he will be served with a summons of removal and deprived of his land.

A factor sent by James Matheson on the island of Lewis in the 1850s.

The 1880s were a period of turmoil in the Highlands with crofters resisting the landlords' wishes. Although the government backed them up with legislation giving them greater rights over their crofts, many crofters continued to leave the Highlands as it was increasingly difficult for the region to support its existing population.

⋯⋮ Activity

1   There are clearly two different views of the Clearances and how they affected the Highlanders. Copy the table below into your notes, inserting rows as necessary, and complete it, using information from the text and sources.

For the Clearances	Against the Clearances

IRISH IMMIGRATION

The 1840s saw an exodus of people from Ireland. Many immigrated to Britain; others to America. This was largely because of their reliance on the potato crop to survive. A blight on the crop had dire consequences for the people of Ireland.

Background

As in the rest of Britain, the population of Ireland was also on the increase and, as there was little industry in Ireland, the population had to rely on the land. However, most of the land in Ireland was owned by the **absentee landlords** from England, so the only way the Irish could get land was to rent it. The demand for land was so high that very often the original tenant sub-let a portion of his land to another and often the sub-tenant would sub-let to a third, and so on. The result of this was a large number of smallholdings. This 'bitty' division of the land made improvement difficult and so few changes occurred, even in basic farming improvements such as crop rotation or hedging and ditching. Even if the landlord himself wanted to make improvements, it was difficult. He would need to evict tenants;

A single-roomed hut in Kildaire, Ireland (*Pictorial Times*, 1870).

this was not popular and if the eviction was challenged, there were often acts of violence against the landlord's agents or cattle.

For those living on the land, the conditions were terrible. Five-sixths of the population lived in single-roomed huts often made of mud.

Since land was scarce, the tenant grew what food he and his family needed, trying to use up the smallest amount of land. Most of this land was used for growing potatoes: this was for very practical reasons. To maintain a family of eight on bread would take up two acres of land, but to maintain a family of eight on potatoes took only one acre. Potatoes were therefore the universal crop and the staple diet of the Irish.

This was all very well until the potato crop came into difficulties, and in the autumn of 1845 the crop was blighted. The situation was critical – people could and did die as a result of this.

Glossary

absentee landlords: landlords who rent out land/property they do not live near.

The blight

In September 1845, a strange disease struck the potatoes as they grew in fields across Ireland. Many of the potatoes were found to have gone black and rotten and their leaves had withered. In the harvest of 1845, between one-third and one-half of the potato crop was destroyed by the strange disease, which became known as 'potato blight'. It was not possible to eat the blighted potatoes and the rest of 1845 was a period of hardship for those who depended on potatoes. The price of potatoes more than doubled over the winter: a hundredweight (50kg) rose in price from 16p to 36p – a huge cost for the ordinary Irish person to bear.

Blighted potatoes have a soggy consistency, smell bad, and are totally inedible. However, the following spring, people continued to plant even more potatoes, thinking that the blight was a one-off and that they would not have to suffer the same hardship in the next winter. By the time the harvest had come in autumn 1846, almost the entire crop had been wiped out.

Source O

As to the potatoes, they are all gone – clean gone. If travelling by night, you would know when a potato field was near by the smell. The fields present a space of withered black stalks.

A priest in Galway in 1846.

The potato blight caused thousands to die not only because of lack of food but because of a lack of affordable food. Many were forced to leave the country.

Source P

Disease and famine have fastened onto the young, the old, the strong and feeble, the mother and the infant; whole families lie together on a damp floor. Without food or fuel, bed or bedding, whole families are shut up in **hovels**, dropping into the arms of death one by one.

An article in the *Cork Examiner* in 1846 describes the plight of the country.

Source Q

A million people deserted their homes to seek for food and shelter in foreign lands. The starving people lived on the dead bodies of diseased cattle, upon dogs and dead horses, but principally on nettle tops, wild mustard and watercress, and even, in some places, dead bodies were found with grass in their mouths …

Census report of 1851 on the famine.

Source R

A Coroner's inquest was held on the lands of Redwood in the parish of Lorha, on yesterday, the 24th, on the body of Daniel Hayes, who for several days subsisted almost on the refuse of vegetables, and went out on the Friday morning in quest of something in the shape of food, but he had not gone far when he was obliged to lie down, and, **melancholy** to relate, was found dead some time afterward.

Cork Examiner, 30 October 1846.

The Prime Minister, Sir Robert Peel, set up a commission of enquiry to try to find out what was causing the potato failures and to suggest ways of preserving good potatoes. The commission was headed by two English scientists, John Lindley and Lyon Playfair. The farmers had already found that the blight thrived in damp weather, and the commission concluded that it was being caused by a form of wet rot. The scientists were unable, however, to find anything that could stop the spread of the blight. It was in 1846 that the first starvations started to happen.

The famine did not affect all of Ireland in the same way. Suffering was most pronounced in the west of Ireland, particularly Connaught, and in the west of Munster. Leinster and especially Ulster escaped more lightly.

Glossary

hovels: small, poorly-built and often dirty houses.

melancholy: sad.

A map of Ireland showing the areas most affected by famine between 1846 and 1849.

There are a number of reasons for this pattern.

- There were distinct kinds of agriculture present in Ireland at the time of the famine. The farmers in the east depended upon cereal crops, while those in Ulster grew flax. Only on the small farms in the west of Ireland, and in parts of Munster, was the potato the main crop. It is estimated that at the eve of the famine 30 per cent of Irish people were largely or wholly dependent on potatoes for their food. As a result, when the blight struck, it was these people who had nothing to fall back on. In Connaught, some have estimated that as many as 25 per cent of the population died.

- City dwellers or those near the cities were also slightly better off – they had more access to imported goods. Dublin, Belfast and Derry escaped with almost no effects at all, while Cork and Wexford were relatively better off than their rural environs. It was the inland and especially the western areas that missed out most from the food of the cities. Given the fact that potatoes are notoriously hard to transport, it would be difficult to get potatoes to Connaught, even in a non-famine situation.

- Many people were also killed by malnutrition-related diseases (such as dysentery and scurvy) and cholera, which swept through the famine-ravaged countryside, as well as by actual starvation. While dysentery is not caused by hunger, recovery depends upon good nutrition. The cholera epidemic was coincidental to the famine and was responsible for a large number of deaths. It was the closely packed west that suffered most from these effects. So the famine was not alone in causing suffering in the 1840s in Ireland.

The effects of the famine

Between 1840 and 1911, the population of Ireland decreased from 8,200,000 to a staggering 4,400,000 as a result of disease, starvation and emigration. As many as a quarter of a million people left Ireland each year, and the famine-related death counts are confirmed at around 750,000, and estimated at about 1,500,000. Many emigrated to America and Britain, often settling in the port towns of these countries. Ireland also lost money in its foreign affairs as it imported five times the amount of grain that it exported.

The welcome the Irish received in Scotland was not always a good one, as Source S below bears out.

Source S

They are landed by their thousands, since the Irish famine, by tens of thousands and just like sheep, at sixpence a head. Our hospitals are filled with them, our police are overwrought by them, our people are robbed and murdered by them.

The Glasgow Herald comments on the new immigrants.

There are many areas where the Irish made an impact on life in Scotland. Many Irish people took up manual labour jobs in industry and in the country; however, they often took a lower wage than the Scots were prepared to and this caused resentment between some Scots and the Irish.

Conflict also grew out of religion. The majority of Irish immigrants in the 1840s were Roman Catholics. The native Protestant population took exception to this and there were many violent incidents due to differences in religion. By the 1870s, many Irish Protestants arrived in Scotland, especially in the west and Glasgow: this caused a further divide between the Protestant and Catholic population.

Generally in society there were problems. Many of the Irish were poor and tended to live together in Irish communities in the poorer areas of the towns. Due to this poverty, many Irish stole and begged to survive and turned to drink for solace. They did not mix with the locals and did not want to send their children to schools that did not guarantee religious teaching. Opinions of the Irish, one of which is found in Source T, were plentiful.

Source T

Enjoying few of the luxuries of life, the people are in general contented, as they are hard working, honest in their dealings, civil, and respectful. The cutting of the canal had at one time a very bad effect upon the character of the population, from the scenes of riot among the Irish labourers.

After the work was finished, a number of Irish took up residence in the village and there was an improvement in their behaviour. Still, however, there is room for improvement in the area of drunkenness, which is the crying evil among the Scottish population.

New Statistical Account for Ratho, Midlothian, 1839.

···> *Activity*

1   Describe the potato blight in Ireland. Make use of the text and other evidence from books or the Internet to give a full description.

2   Use the information in the text to write a paragraph to explain the effects of the potato famine on Ireland as a whole and on different areas in Ireland.

... IN CONCLUSION

···> ■ The population in Scotland and Britain not only increased but moved.

■ Cities grew and the countryside had fewer people.

■ Due to changes in farming, thousands of Highlanders left their homeland to settle in the Lowlands or overseas.

■ The period known as the Highland Clearances was when people were evicted from their crofts and replaced by sheep or deer farming.

■ Many who left the Highlands settled in the cities in the Lowlands of Scotland or emigrated overseas to America and Canada.

■ The blight on the potato crop caused hardship and starvation for the Irish poor, a situation which meant that thousands left Ireland to go to Britain and America.

PRACTISE YOUR ENQUIRY SKILLS

Study the sources in this chapter carefully and answer the questions that follow. You should use your own knowledge where appropriate.

1   How useful do you think Source F on page 11 is for giving information about the population in the 1800s?

2   In what ways does Source E on page 10 agree with Source F on page 11 about changes in the population?

3   How useful is Source G on page 12 as evidence of the Clearances?

4   What is the attitude of Francis Clark in Source L on page 13 towards the Clearances?

5   How valuable is Source P on page 16 as evidence of the effects of the blight?

6   How fully does Source Q on page 16 describe the effects of the blight on people's lives? Use evidence from the source and your own knowledge to answer this question.

7   How reliable is Source T on page 18 as evidence of the reaction of Scots to the Irish immigrants?

8 How useful is this cartoon as evidence of the potato blight?

9 The issue for investigating is:

Changes in farming brought about the biggest movement to the population in the nineteenth century.

Study the sources carefully and answer the questions that follow. You should use your own knowledge where appropriate.

Source U is from the *Aberdeen Herald*, 1852.

Source U

> The cold and damp bothy without a fire 'till the men light it, dishes unwashed, stepping stones to wade over pools of mud, the everlasting food of meal and milk will not persuade young ploughmen to stay and give up their chance of comfort in America or Australia.

A cartoon from the *Illustrated London News* in 1849, showing starving people searching for potatoes.

Source V is a description by an inhabitant of Glasgow in 1838.

Source V

> There are people who have come to Glasgow from as far as 60 miles away. My own father was a farmer in the Lothians. He was driven out by improvements in farming, so he became a mechanic and settled in Glasgow. When small farms disappeared, many cottagers were driven out and they moved to large towns.

a) How useful is Source U in providing reasons for people leaving their homes?

b) What evidence is there to support the view that farming changes were a factor in people leaving their homes?

c) What evidence is there to support the view that there were other reasons for people wanting to leave their homes?

d) To what extent do you think that changes in farming were the main reason for people leaving their homes in the nineteenth century? You must use evidence from the sources and your own knowledge to reach a balanced conclusion.

ANSWERING A KNOWLEDGE AND UNDERSTANDING QUESTION

Source W is taken from the New Statistical Account for Dundee in 1833.

Source W

> The cause of this extraordinary increase in population is due to the great growth of the linen trade, which has produced so many spinning mills. By giving employment to thousands it has encouraged early marriages (and more children), as well as bringing families from other parts of Scotland and from Ireland.

1   **Describe why the population between 1830 and 1900 grew. Use all of Source W and any recalled knowledge.**

Answer

At the start of the 1800s most people lived in the countryside; by the end of this period the towns were much larger and more densely populated. The population had also grown dramatically due to people marrying younger and having more children. In areas such as Newbattle in East Lothian, the attraction was the coal mining industry where the whole family could be employed. In Dundee it was the linen trade that offered employment and thus the opportunity to marry earlier. The population in the towns also grew because families were moving into the country from Ireland and the Highlands of Scotland. Many changes in health and medicine also meant people were living much longer.

Comment

The candidate gives a balanced answer with knowledge and information taken from the source as well as recalled knowledge. In all, there are three points from the source and four from recall. A marker would expect to see both demonstrated in an answer. Here, the answer shows clearly that the question has been answered properly and that the candidate has a clear knowledge of the topic in question.

EXTENDED WRITING PRACTICE

1   Do you think the movement of the people from the Highlands in the 1800s was justified?

You should consider:

■   the views and evidence of the crofters

■   the views and evidence of the landowners.

You should include a conclusion that provides a balanced answer to the question.

2   In pairs, read over all the information you have so far about population change in Scotland. Decide which factors are important. Explain why so many people moved to the large towns in the nineteenth century. Prepare your answer so that it can be presented to the rest of the class – you can do this using PowerPoint, a display poster or any format you feel at ease with.

2 LIVING AND WORKING IN THE COUNTRYSIDE

How did farming change between the 1830s and the 1930s?

What's it all about?

Between 1830 and 1930, the face of farming changed dramatically. The methods and style of farming changed in such a way that the landscape of Britain altered its appearance. Technology in farming developed and new ideas swept the land.

Enclosures

For centuries, the British countryside had looked the same – it featured open field farming where families farmed strips of land – but by the 1800s this had been revolutionised and the countryside transformed.

Farming in strips meant that a farmer would move from one area (strip) of his land to another, cultivating each strip so that he was able to produce enough for his needs. The old system of farming using open field strips (runrigs in Scotland) had been adequate for the population at the time, but by the 1800s the population was growing and the demand for farmers to grow more food increased. Out went the age-old scattered strips and in came enclosed farms.

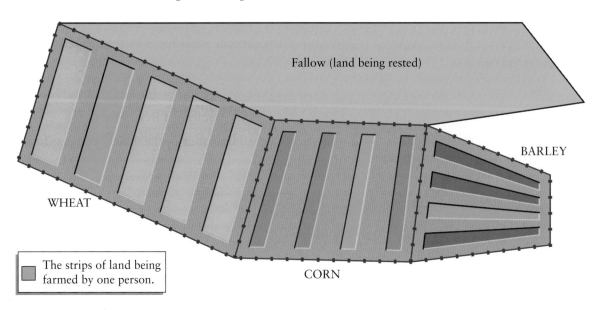

Fallow (land being rested)

BARLEY

WHEAT

CORN

The strips of land being farmed by one person.

Strip farming. In this example, one farmer has a strip of wheat, a strip of corn and a strip of barley.

Percentage of farmland in Britain enclosed in the eighteenth and nineteenth centuries.

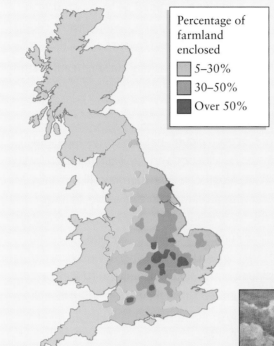

Percentage of farmland enclosed
- 5–30%
- 30–50%
- Over 50%

Source A

All I know is that I had a cow and an Act of Parliament has taken it from me.

A labourer from the 1800s.

FURTHER CHANGES TO FARMING

The changes to the way the land was divided encouraged change. Implements, which had hardly changed for years, were no longer efficient and effective on the new larger fields. So the new farms led to new methods of farming and new machines such as the seed drill, the horse-pulled plough, **marling** soil and a more scientific approach to the breeding of animals.

The old system, which had wasted land, time and labour, was replaced over the years by larger farms, which could produce more crops more effectively. Land was no longer divided up: hedges and fences were put around fields and enclosed. The drawback of this system was that for many families with smallholdings it meant losing land or having to sell to wealthier landowners and moving to the new towns. If the owners of four-fifths of the land agreed, they could force the rest to comply via an Act of Parliament. So, not everyone was happy: one opinion is shown in Source A.

The horse-drawn plough was one of the new methods of farming (engraving by W. H. Hopkins, 1882).

Men such as Jethro Tull and Viscount 'Turnip' Townshend became well known. They knew that the **fallow** field was unnecessary and that scientific crop rotation would lead to fields being able to produce better crops. Townshend introduced a four-year cycle of wheat, turnip, barley (or oats) and clover rotation – each crop replaced the goodness in the soil the previous one had taken out. Turnip and clover introduced nitrogen, which acted as a fertiliser into the soil.

Glossary

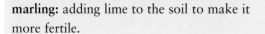

marling: adding lime to the soil to make it more fertile.

fallow: left unseeded for a period of time after ploughing to allow soil to recover.

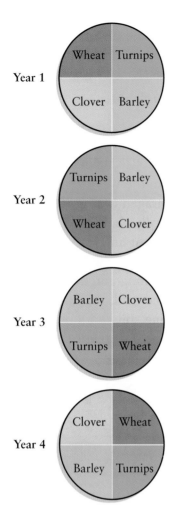

Year 1	Wheat / Turnips / Clover / Barley

Year 2	Turnips / Barley / Wheat / Clover

Year 3	Barley / Clover / Turnips / Wheat

Year 4	Clover / Wheat / Barley / Turnips

A four-year crop rotation.

Root crops such as turnips also improved efficiency by providing winter food for cattle and sheep. A more scientific way of breeding animals was also adopted so that animals would produce better meat.

There were many changes in farming methods during this period and these new ideas spread throughout the land. The Board of Agriculture was set up with Arthur Young as the new Secretary. He travelled throughout the country taking note of the changes being made and sharing the information about the benefits of the new farming methods and Enclosures.

Source B

The benefit of enclosing the land can be seen in Lincoln Heath. It used to be covered with weeds, but now it is used as farmland. People can earn a good living from the land.

Arthur Young, after visiting Lincoln Heath in 1813.

Source C

The 'Scotch plough' has all but disappeared from this district and has been replaced by the chain plough. One man can now **till** the same field with a team of horses as would have previously required the work of six men and the same number of oxen. Skilled ploughmen are much wanted by the farmers and can earn enough in the ploughing season to support their families throughout the winter months.

A Survey of the Agriculture of the County of Ayrshire, 1843.

Glossary

till: to prepare the land for growing crops by ploughing.

THE EFFECTS OF ENCLOSURES

On the whole, the effects of the Enclosure system were notable. The countryside changed in appearance, with large new farmhouses being built and small villages becoming depopulated. Open fields had given way to compact farms with hedges and ditches. More land was cultivated and animals became fatter. It also became easier to experiment with different ways of farming. The wastefulness of the runrig system was removed and the profits of many farmers increased.

However, many people lost their jobs and had to move away from the countryside to find work in the towns. This also caused a decline in many of the old skills and customs in the countryside.

Source D

The decreased population here is due to the uniting of the rigs into enlarged farms so that fewer hands are needed, and so many have gone to the towns.

Arthur Young, describing the population in the countryside in the 1830s.

Source E

The law arrests the man or woman
Who steals the goose from the common,
But leaves the greater rascal loose,
Who steals the common from the goose.

A popular rhyme of the eighteenth century reflects the view of some people at the time.

In many instances, the rich farmers were the winners, gaining large productive farms at the expense of those who were less wealthy.

1 Explain in your own words how the system of strip farming worked.

2 Make a chart to show the advantages and disadvantages of strip farming like the one below.

Strip farming	
Advantages	Disadvantages

3 Make a chart to show the advantages and disadvantages of the Enclosures like the one below.

Enclosures	
Advantages	Disadvantages

4 Were the Enclosures a good change or not? Write a paragraph for your answer, which reaches a conclusion. Make use of the text and source information.

THE GOLDEN AGE

The 1830s to the 1870s were known as the 'Golden Age' of British agriculture. Food prices were high and so most farmers had little difficulty in paying their rents and bills. Changes in attitudes to the economy made a difference. The 1830s and 1840s had been the era of the Corn Laws, which prohibited foreign corn coming into Britain until British corn reached a high enough price for the farmers. These laws had ensured that while the farmers had a reasonable profit, the price of bread remained high. In 1846, the government decided to remove or repeal these laws to allow cheap corn into the country. This was partly due to the impact of the famine in Ireland.

Farmers were hardly affected by the repeal of the Corn Laws. New inventions and farming improvements helped increase production to the extent that it beat off foreign competition.

Selective breeding of animals was improved in this period. Pastoral farming seemed to become more popular than **arable** farming. New breeds such as the Lincoln sheep produced by Bakewell, Aberdeen Angus beef cattle, and the Suffolk Punch workhorse had an impact on farming.

Farmers were keen to invest money in improving and reorganising farming to improve efficiency. Drainage was improved allowing more land to be farmed. Steam-powered machines were also being produced to **thresh**, remove **chaff** and cut crops as well as plough.

The Golden Age came to an abrupt end in the early 1870s: a succession of wet summers and bad harvests, combined with cattle and sheep disease, led to a depression for farmers. The new technology that had been developed was being used abroad, and overseas suppliers such as America could supply as quickly and cheaply as the home market. As a result, British agriculture was in crisis. British farmers were forced to concentrate on dairy and beef production, which could not be so readily out-done by foreign competition.

A combined steam threshing and stacking machine made in Boston, Lincolnshire (*Illustrated London News* 1861).

1   List three reasons for the 'Golden Age' of agriculture.

2   Explain why the 'Golden Age' of agriculture ended in the 1870s. (Give three reasons.)

Glossary

arable: farming mainly cultivating crops.

thresh: to separate the seeds of a plant from the straw.

chaff: the dry covering of grain.

POST-1880S FARMING

The start of the twentieth century saw a change in government attitude to farming. The government preferred to provide cheap food for the population and this came from overseas. Moreover, the focus of the government was more on industry rather than agriculture. By 1914, Britain imported almost 60 per cent of all its foodstuffs.

The year 1914, at the outbreak of the First World War, was crucial for Britain and agriculture. The war highlighted the dangers of importing food from overseas. Shipping was a target for German submarines, particularly those vessels carrying food and raw materials. By 1917, the Germans had almost succeeded in starving Britain into surrender, and the government was forced to introduce food rationing and to provide subsidies for bread and potatoes. This was even with the huge impact the Women's Land Army was making on the attempts to keep the country fed. At its peak, the Land Army reached a cohort of some 16,000 women, but with the end of the war many left their land work.

Post-war Britain saw even greater depressions in farming – subsidies were removed and the farmers were left to struggle with falling prices and foreign competition. In Scotland, between 1921 and 1938, the number of farm workers fell from 126,900 to 105,300.

WORKING CONDITIONS ON THE LAND

Many farm workers were unhappy with their working conditions in the 1830s. They were poorly paid: a wage of around 35 to 40 pence per week. Their work was physically demanding as well as involving long hours. Much of their work was also outside, no matter what the weather was like, and with few machines at this time, it involved long and often unpleasant working conditions. There were no unions as such for farm workers, so employers could sack workers without any warning. Many labourers worked on a day-to-day basis. Often the farm workers lived in tied houses, in other words, houses that went with the job. It meant that if you lost your job, you also lost your home. Rents were high and the quality of housing not good. Workers were reluctant to complain to the farmers or join trade unions in case they lost their jobs and homes.

Even with improvements in the 'Golden Age' in particular, farming still remained a tough job. Men, women and children all worked in the fields. It was not until 1872 that the Agricultural Labourers' Union was set up. It fought for better wages and conditions for farm workers, but the threat of being sacked was always there for anyone who joined it, so the union was weak.

⋯⋄ Activity

Working in groups, discuss all the good and bad points of the introduction of Enclosures. List them using evidence from texts and any other sources you can find. Decide as a group whether you are for or against the Enclosures. Write a speech to convince others of your group's point of view. Write it in such a way that it can become part of a class debate entitled: 'The Enclosures were the best thing that could have happened to farming in the nineteenth century.'

LIVING CONDITIONS ON THE LAND

In the days before major improvement, buildings were strictly functional: they were built with local materials, and in the Highlands that meant stone, clay, turf and heather, as well as the most valuable part, timber, for the roofing.

Accommodation

In the 1830s, conditions for farms were basic. Workers or 'Cottars' lived in single-roomed houses with basic conditions. As farming improved so, too, did some of the accommodation, with rows of houses being built for farm workers. In the Highlands, the accommodation was more unique, taking on the look and materials local to the area.

Shielings

Many of the smaller buildings were used as shielings. These were seasonal houses, often in higher pastures, where families would take their cattle for the best grazing. These shielings were built in groups next to streams and lochs. The earliest examples were shaped like beehives and made from turf and stone.

Shielings in Uig, Scotland, 1800s (*Scottish Pictures* 1886).

Source F

And then in May we went to the shielings, at least we did. At one time, everybody did, but latterly … my mother had the last shieling in the village because she believed shieling life was good for man and beast. So we went about the first day of May and came home the last Friday in July. So I had to run to school four miles every morning and four miles back at night.

Donald MacDonald of Tolsta in Lewis describes his experiences of the shielings on his young life.

The blackhouse

By the nineteenth century, the buildings became more rectangular in shape and became known as blackhouses. A blackhouse had a double wall with turf in between the two walls. The roof was a wooden frame, which rested on the inside half of the wall, leaving a ledge wide enough for a man to walk along. Over the frame was an overlapping layer of heathery **turves** and over this a layer of thatch was laid. This would then be secured by old fishing net or twine attached to large stones, which would weigh everything down.

Traditionally, the roof had no chimney – smoke had to find its own way out of the house. The fire was lit at all times so that the thatch would not rot and also because smoked thatch was considered an excellent fertiliser. The thatch was removed each year for this purpose and the blackhouse re-thatched. The crofters had few possessions – everything had to have a practical use.

Glossary

turves: plural of turf.

Layer of thatch

Twine

Double walls

Layer of heathery turves

Wooden frame roof resting on inside of the double wall

Turf

The structure of a nineteenth-century blackhouse.

A blackhouse with 'modern' additions (windows and chimney).

The animals would be at one end of the house and the byre area had earth flooring with a drain for waste. Part of the house would also be used for storage.

Source G

The blackhouse of a century or so ago was a grim and unprepossessing dwelling. Its walls were perpetually damp. It had no windows and no chimney, the smoke from the fire that burned perpetually in one corner being left to find its way out through a hole in the roof. The floor was trampled mud; the furniture virtually non-existent.

The crofter's cattle lived under the same straw-thatched, leaking roof as the crofter and his family. Beast and humans entered by the same door.

In these dark, dank, unsanitary and foul-smelling homes, typhoid and cholera persisted long after they had been eradicated in many other parts of Britain. And that most dreaded of island diseases, tuberculosis, haunted the blackhouse well into the present century.

James Hunter of Skye, 1970s.

There are only a few blackhouses standing today – the Clearances, decay and agricultural improvement have reduced many to ruins. Although they had many disadvantages, they suited the weather and made good use of the resources to hand. By the 1850s, many landlords rebuilt and improved cottages left on the land, but this was at the cost of higher rents without an increase in wages.

> Describe a shieling and its uses.

···⁖ Activity

Imagine you are an architect. You have been asked to design a blackhouse for the twentieth century. Make a table listing the old features of the blackhouse and next to each one the changes you would make with an explanation as to why you would do this.

Monymusk House, Aberdeenshire is an example of a wealthy landowner's house (J. W. Giles 1848).

Other Highland housing

Blackhouses and shielings were not the only types of housing in the Highlands. Farmers who farmed large areas of land lived in two-storey homes with slate roofs. The wealthier landowners had huge dwellings, often like castles, with several rooms and a squad of servants to look after the family and the grounds of the house.

... IN CONCLUSION

- The increasing population meant that new farming methods had to be found.
- Enclosing the land meant not as many people were needed to farm the land but more food was produced.
- Changes in farming resulted in new technologies being used.
- The 1830s–70s was the 'Golden Age' for British farming.
- During the First World War, women began to play an even bigger role in farming, only for farming to experience a further depression in the 1920s and 1930s.
- Much of the housing in the Highlands was basic and built of local materials.
- Improvements did take place after the 1850s.
- Wealthier farmers had better housing.

PRACTISE YOUR ENQUIRY SKILLS

Study the sources in this chapter carefully and answer the questions that follow. You should use your own knowledge where appropriate.

1 Read Source A on page 23 carefully. What does the author think about enclosing land? Explain your answer with reference to the source.

2 How reliable do you think Source C on page 24 is about the impact of new machines on farming?

3 To what extent do Sources C, D and E on pages 24 and 25 agree about the effects of the Enclosures?

4 How useful is Source F on page 28 as evidence of shieling life?

5 Which do you consider more valuable as evidence about the blackhouses: the diagram on page 28, or Source G? Give reasons for your answers.

ANSWERING A KNOWLEDGE AND UNDERSTANDING QUESTION

Question

Source H is from *Farmlife in Northeast Scotland 1840–1914* by Ian Carter (1979).

Source H

> There has been great improvement in the condition of the ploughmen's cottages during the past 25 years. Many of them at that time contained only one big room subdivided by the furniture of two box beds and a chest of drawers and cupboard combined. The floors are generally of earth or clay.

1 Describe the housing of people in the countryside in the nineteenth century.

In the answer below recall information has been highlighted.

Answer

In the countryside, people made use of local resources to build their homes. Blackhouses and shielings were the most common homes in the countryside. The houses made of turf and stone were made up of one large room with basic furniture, that is, beds and drawers. The floor was trampled down earth. The fire was inside and smoke had to find its own way out as there was no chimney. Often the animals shared the houses with the people.

Comments

This answer uses information both from the source itself and from recalled knowledge to give a well-balanced response to the question. In all, there are two points from the source and six points from recalled knowledge. An examiner would expect to see both demonstrated in a good answer. This mix of recalled knowledge and information taken from the source demonstrates that the candidate understands the question and has a clear knowledge of the topic.

3   COAL MINING

What was the role of coal in British industry?

What's it all about?

In this chapter you will learn the reasons for the demand for coal, and about early mines as well as the development of more modern mines. You will also learn about working in the coal mines and the dangers it involved, and changes in mining over time, including the impact of the First World War.

WHY WAS COAL SO IMPORTANT?

Central to the running of industry was coal: it was the fuel of the time. Between 1830 and 1910, the production of coal rose from 30 million tons to 270 million with over 1 million miners working in 1910. The effects of the increased demand for coal had a great impact on conditions in the mines and the development of new mining technologies.

Reasons for the demand for coal

The biggest demand for coal came via the need for steam to power the engines and machines of industry.

Steam power, produced through coal, was needed to run the railways, steam ships and the machines of the textile factories. Coal was also turned into coke to smelt iron in furnaces throughout the country. In the home, people were also using coal more and more for heating, and as time progressed, coal was used in gas production for street and house lighting. Most of the mines in Scotland were in the Central Belt, Ayrshire, Fife and Lothian.

As a result, new pits were opened, which went deeper than ever before to try to get the greatest amount of coal out of the ground. Thus, as the demand for coal increased, so did the demands and dangers faced by the miners.

Distribution of the main coal fields in nineteenth century Scotland.

Early mines

Early mines were bell pits owned or used by a few men.

A bell pit coal mine in Ireland.

The mines developed into an underground world of tunnels and routes, hundreds of feet beneath the ground, where coal was hacked from the seam and carried along and up the tunnels to the surface.

Working in the mines

As the mines got deeper, so the jobs became increasingly dangerous; there was always the risk of roofs caving in, explosions, floods, fires or escaping poisonous gases. With plenty of people looking for work, the mine owners were able to employ cheap labour to bring as much coal to the surface as possible for maximum profit. Whole families worked in the mines with a lot of the work underground being carried out by women and children, including a lot of the heavy cutting and carrying of the coal. The owners did nothing to improve safety – this would cost them money and with plenty of people looking for employment, workers could easily be replaced. The government of the time took the attitude of '*laissez-faire*' and left things alone.

Glossary

laissez-faire: French for 'leave alone', a government view of not becoming involved in social or economic issues.

Trappers

The youngest children, some as young as four or five, worked as trappers, opening and shutting the traps on the air doors of the mines. The air doors were an attempt to keep the air in the mines clean. The trappers sat in the pitch dark, opening the doors when they heard either a truck or people wanting to get to another part of the mine.

ladder

'trapper' opening trapdoor, which controlled ventilation

'bearer' raising coal

300/600ft deep

'drawer' pulling coal

'hewer' cutting coal

The work of hewers, drawers, trappers and bearers in a mine of the 1830s.

Source A

I stand and open and shut the door; I am generally in the dark and sit down against the door; I stop twelve hours in the pit; I never see daylight, except on Sunday; I fell asleep one day and a **corve** ran over my leg and made it smart (hurt).

A trapper describes his work in 1842.

Hewers

Hewers were mainly men or older boys who cut the coal away from the coal face. It was a dangerous and tiring job.

Source B

I have worked below ground for three years, except when I was injured. A pick struck a piece of metal and cast sparks and cost me the loss of my eye. I go down at five in the morning and come away about seven at night … The part of the pit I work in is very wet and I am obliged to sit on a wet bit of coal to keep the water off.

James Ward describes his job as a hewer in 1842.

Children hauling coal past a trapdoor (1842).

Bearers

Once the coal had been cut by the hewers it was put in carts, which were dragged or pushed to the bottom of the pit shaft. The boys and girls who carried out this job often had belts round their waists and a chain between their legs and crawled along the narrow pit seams. As with all jobs, shifts were long and dangerous. Other 'coal bearers' carried loads of coal on their backs in big baskets.

Source C

I have been working below three years on my father's account; he takes me down at two in the morning, and I come up at one or two the next afternoon. I go to bed at six to be ready for work the next morning: in my part of the pit I bear (carry) my burden up four traps, or ladders, before I get to the main road, which leads to the pit bottom. My task is four or five tubs; each tub holds four and a quarter cwt. I fill five tubs in twenty journeys. I have had the strap when I did not do my bidding. Am very glad when my task is wrought (over), as it sore fatigues.

Ellison Jack, an eleven-year-old girl, who worked at Loanhead Colliery (Mine) (1842).

Source D

The collier population is subject to a peculiar disease, which is **vulgarly** called black-spit. It is a wasting of the lungs caused by the inhaling of the coal dust while working and the **expectoration** is as black as the coal dust itself. Many strong men are cut off by it before they reach the age of 40 … Almost all men are affected by it sooner or later.

1840 Statistical Account of Edinburgh.

Glossary

corve: coal truck.

vulgarly: commonly, rudely.

expectoration: spit or phlegm.

In the 1840s, the government decided to investigate conditions in mines and compiled a report. This was based on evidence gathered by a Royal Commission, whose members spoke to owners as well as the men, women and children who worked in the mines. Opinions differed as to what life was like in the mines for the workers. Some owners complained to the government about the report. The most famous opponent of the report was the Marquis of Londonderry. He owned a particularly rich mine in the north-east of England and went as far as organising a petition to complain.

Source E

Trappers are neither cheerless or dull; nor are they kept alone and in darkness all the time. Trappers are generally cheerful and happy.

Marquis of Londonderry in 1842.

Despite this protest, the Coal Mining Act 1842 was passed. This banned women and children under the age of ten from working in the mines and one inspector (for all of Britain) was appointed to monitor the **legislation**. Unfortunately, he did not have the power to go down pits until 1850! It was also difficult to check up on the ages of children working underground and parents were not keen to lose out on a wage earner. There was also no mention of the dreadful working conditions of men and boys over ten.

However, at least the Act was a step in the right direction, not only for mines but other industries as well.

Things were still far from perfect after 1842.

Glossary

legislation: laws.

FURTHER LEGISLATION

1855	Safety rules had to be drawn up by each colliery.
1860	Boys under the age of twelve were not allowed underground unless they could read or write.
1862	Safety rules regarding ventilation and mine exits; mines had to have an emergency exit in case of accident.
1872	Mine managers had to pass an exam to say they were competent. Also, mine workers could appoint their own safety manager.
1909	The eight-hour-a-day rule was brought in for those working underground.
1911	Baths had to be available at the pithead for miners.
1917	The working day was reduced to seven hours a day.

Despite legislation, accidents in the mines were still common. The deeper the mines, the more dangerous they became with the ever-present risk of flooding, cave-ins and gas.

Source F

The traditions of miners, the slow pace of change and the fear of unemployment, all combined to lead the miner to regard the introduction of machinery with sometimes open hostility. They hated every minute of the unpleasant work, clearing away the rock and the coal from the cutting tool and putting in wooden gibs to support the undercut coal. Machine setting teams had to face high noise levels and thick choking dust. No masks were issued.

A Lanarkshire miner in 1842.

The 1880s through to the outbreak of war in 1914 saw a record amount of coal being exported from Britain, but there was no great change in the number of accidents that occurred in the mines. Even as late as the early 1920s, almost 600,000 miners were injured underground.

In the following years, many improvements took place: many mine owners did try to take account of technological developments.

Source G

The opening of the Lady Victoria pit at Newbattle Colliery, which began in 1890, started a new era in mineral development in the two counties. The pumping, winding and haulage engines are all of the latest type.

S. Black, a retired engineer, in *Mining in Mid and East Lothian*, published in 1925.

In 1914, most of the coal cutting was still being done by hand. However, by 1928, 60 per cent was being cut mechanically.

1   Why did coal become so important by the 1800s?

2   List the various jobs carried out in the coal mines in the 1800s. Write a short description of each job stating who would have carried out the job and what the job involved.

3   Describe the dangers faced by those who worked in the mines in the nineteenth century.

4   What dangers did new technology bring in?

⋯⋗ *Activity*

Review the legislation that was introduced between 1842 and 1917. Imagine you are a miner in 1917: write a letter to your local MP saying what other laws you think could be brought in to improve your working conditions.

THE COAL INDUSTRY AND THE FIRST WORLD WAR

The First World War had a huge impact on the coal industry. By the end of the first year of the war – 1914 – there was a serious drop in the amount of coal being mined. This was largely due to the number of miners who volunteered for the armed forces.

However, coal was essential for the war – it was needed for factories, iron works for weapons, railways and ships. There was thus still a great demand for coal. With fewer miners at the coal face, the owners knew they had to try to do something to increase production. Their initial solution was to try to increase working hours. This was resisted by the miners.

By July of 1915, the output from the coal industry was down by 3 million tons per month. Something fairly drastic had to be done to ensure that there was enough coal to keep the country going. In February 1917, Prime Minister David Lloyd George announced that the mines would be run by the state for the duration of the conflict, which meant that the state would control the output and distribution of coal. Miners were now no longer able to join the army. In many cases, their wages were higher than they had been during peacetime. The war work in the coal industry was acknowledged as just as crucial as the troops fighting in France. This had an impact on the future of ownership of mines.

Source H

In the opinion of this Conference, the time has come when this country should no longer be run by a small group of capitalist coal owners, coal dealers and merchants. The consumer is made to pay a quite unnecessary price for coal due to the combinations of these groups. The government should at once take over all coal and other mines, and work with them as a national enterprise.

Motion put before the Annual Conference of Scottish Miners in August 1918.

In the years after the wars, laws were passed to try to improve safety and conditions further – hours were cut to seven a day and pithead baths were put in place. However, the mining industry was still faced with problems. Cheap coal was being imported from Poland and Germany and less coal was being exported. Alternative fuels such as oil were being developed and less coal was needed in some of the larger industries such as the steel industry.

In 1921, the mines were returned to their former owners and this caused great conflict among the miners, many of whom wanted the mines to be fully **nationalised**. Further conflict grew when owners tried to cut wages. After striking for one month, the miners returned to work. Trouble in the mines continued in 1925 when owners tried to increase the working day by an hour and decrease miners' wages. The miners did not accept this and fought using the slogan 'Not a minute on the day, not a penny off the pay'. On 3 May 1926, they joined the General Strike with other heavy industries. This lasted nine days, but the miners stayed out for six months. In the end, they had to accept pay cuts and an increase in hours.

In 1947, the mines were eventually **nationalised**.

Glossary

nationalised: run and owned by the government.

Miners staging a 'sit-down' strike outside Prestpans Colliery, East Lothian during the General Strike of 1926.

1   Explain the effects of the First World War on the mining industry.

2   What action did the Scottish miners want the government to take regarding the ownership of the coal industry? Explain why you think they took this point of view.

···꞉ Activity

1   Working with a partner, try to find out about the technological improvements that started to be used in the mines in the period 1830–1930. Use the Internet and other resources available to you. Present your findings using the following table.

Name of equipment	Date introduced	Improvement it made to mining

2   Working in groups of three or four, create a poster to illustrate the effects of one of the new technologies on the mines. Your poster should include the following information:

■ what the new or improved technology was

■ what impact the new technology had at the coal face

■ an evaluation of how the new technology affected the mining industry.

··· In Conclusion

···꞉ ■ Mining grew with the changes in industry and the need for power.

■ Children and women worked underground until 1842.

■ Conditions did not improve much despite legislation and new technologies underground.

■ The impact of the First World War changed the face of the coal industry so that it became nationalised by 1947.

PRACTISE YOUR ENQUIRY SKILLS

**Study the sources in this chapter carefully and answer the questions that follow.
You should use your own knowledge where appropriate.**

The issue for investigating is:

Safety in coal mining had improved by the 1930s.

Source I was written in 1869 by David Bremner. He wrote about a visit he had made to
Arniston Coal Mine in Midlothian in the 1840s.

Source I

> The miners enter the pit between five and six o'clock in the morning. They are in
> constant danger of a violent death or injury. The winding gear may give way and there
> are the dangers of being suffocated by foul air or being scorched to death by the
> ignition of the damp (methane). In 1865 in Scotland, 12,034,638 tons of coal were
> raised and 77 lives lost.

Source J is from 'A Short History of the Scottish Coal Mining Industry', published by the
National Coal Board in 1958.

Source J

> By the 1930s, there had been great progress in power machinery which cut and
> loaded the coal mechanically. This meant that mining could be carried out efficiently
> and with greater safety and that made for greater productivity than in the days of
> pick, shovel and pit ponies.

1   How useful is Source I as evidence about conditions in the mines in the 1800s?

2   What evidence in Source I agrees with the view that miners still faced dangers in the 1860s?
    What evidence in Source J disagrees with the view that miners still faced dangers by the 1930s?

3   How far do you agree that safety in coal mining had improved by the 1930s?
    Use evidence in the sources and your own knowledge to come to a conclusion.

ANSWERING AN ENQUIRY SKILLS QUESTION

Question

1   **How useful is Source G on page 36 as evidence of investment in new mining?**

Answer

Source G provides useful evidence of investment mining for many reasons.

- ⋯▷ *Who?* The quote is from a specialist book written by a retired engineer.
- ⋯▷ *What?* The basis of his knowledge is his own experience and
- ⋯▷ *Why?* as an eye-witness he would be aware of changes that took place over the years in the mining industry.
- ⋯▷ *When?* Published in 1925,
- ⋯▷ *Should we trust it?* it has the benefit of hindsight enabling him to look at the past with impartial eyes. He will, of course, have put his own view into this, but he has obviously a great insight into coal mining and changes during the period. He would also be aware of all the latest developments and so be able easily, at a glance, to identify the latest technology.

Comments

Here, the candidate has analysed the source in a systematic way and this results in a clear and thorough answer. The candidate starts by looking at who the source is written by and how this affects the quality of the information in the source. The candidate goes on to look at the content of the source, including any possible bias, before reaching a conclusion as to whether the source is useful as evidence of investment in new mining.

4 THE EXPANSION OF THE RAILWAYS

Railways: a good development for Britain?

What's it all about?

In this chapter you will learn about the development of the railways and what was involved in building them. You will discover the impact the railways had on everyday life in Britain, and assess both the positive and negative reactions that people had to the introduction of a railway system.

The mid to late 1800s saw many changes taking place, not least of which were in the system of transport used throughout the country. As changes and progress were being made in industry, so, too, a new transport system emerged. The need for a fast and efficient transport system to move goods encouraged the development of new transport in the form of the railways.

THE DEVELOPMENT OF THE RAILWAYS

The idea of using rails to speed up transport was not new to the 1800s – horse-driven trucks had been pulled along wooden tracks in the coal mines for years. Initially, therefore, simple wooden rail tracks were used for early steam engines. In 1805, a wooden rail link ran from Troon to Kilmarnock, but as technology advanced the wooden tracks were soon replaced by iron. In 1812, the first railway, which used a George Stephenson steam locomotive, was authorised by Parliament.

Horses pulling rail trucks in the Staffordshire colliery of Bradley, 1869.

George Stephenson's 'Rocket' (19th century engraving).

The first public line opened in Scotland in 1826 with the Monkland and Kirkintilloch railway, which used steam and horse traction. The development of faster and more efficient trains increased the demand for railway lines to link up towns and cities throughout the land. In 1842, the Edinburgh to Glasgow line opened up with many others following quickly behind. This was going to have a huge impact on life in Britain: not only did the railways allow people and goods to move from one end of the country to the other but it also created jobs, made goods cheaper and had a lasting effect on the countryside.

With such changes it was inevitable that an alternative to horse power would be used to try to speed up the system. There were early experiments with steam engines, for example, Puffing Billy in 1814, but it is generally George Stephenson who is credited as the principal inventor of the railway locomotive and who is often known as the 'Father of the Railways'. Railway transport was really born on 27 September 1825 when Stephenson's *Locomotion* ran from Darlington to Stockton, carrying 450 people at fifteen miles per hour (24km/h). In 1830, Stephenson's later *Rocket* won a famous competition to find the fastest locomotive by travelling at an average speed of 36 miles per hour (58km/h) from Liverpool to Manchester. Stephenson also played a huge part in 'Railway Mania', when everyone became aware of the railways and they became hugely popular.

A map of England, Wales and southern Scotland showing the railway network in 1852.

1   Describe the early trains.

2   What development led to railways being thought of as a more useful method of transport?

A map of England, Wales and southern Scotland showing the railway network in 1921.

The years between 1830 and 1850 in particular saw the opening of many railway lines throughout the country.

Year	Miles of railway line
1830	69
1840	1857
1850	6621
1860	10,433
1870	15,557

With more lines and faster locomotives, safety also became an issue – a man standing on the line waving a flag to stop trains was too dangerous! While the first railway saw many accidents – including train collisions and people jumping off moving trains – trains soon became the safest mode of transport in Britain as improvements were made using guards, semaphore signals and the telegraph.

Write a paragraph to explain why and how railways developed in the 1800s. Use information from other sources.

⋯ Activity

Design an 1840s advertising poster to encourage people to make use of this new form of transport. Mention all the good points about railway travel and how it is going to impact on people's lives.

You may want to target certain groups of people in your poster, for example, holiday travellers, market traders, and so on.

REACTIONS TO THE RAILWAYS

Reactions to the railways varied.

Source B

Railways will mean that all parts of the country will become more opened up, land in the interior will, by a system of cheap and rapid transport for manure and farm produce, became almost as valuable as land on the coast. The man of business can easily join his family at a distance of ten or twelve miles as could formerly be done at two or three miles.

An article in the *Scottish Railway Gazette*, April 1845.

Private land had to be bought by the railway companies if they wanted their line to go on a particular route – this often caused problems.

Source C is part of an interview with Maytone Graham of Cultoquey about the effects of the railways on the Saughton Hall Estate in 1841.

Source C

Do you know Saughton Hall?
Yes.

Is it benefited in any way by the railway?
No.

Is it injured?
I do say it is enormously injured.

Before the railway was made, was it a compact and most desirable estate?
For its size I do not know a more compact or more desirable estate were the railway away from it.

Is the character of it changed and the power of the proprietors over it lessened?
It has changed – its unity destroyed, and it is divided into two portions very incorrectly, particularly for the bottom part.

Is the amenity of the Estate destroyed?
Its amenity is very much injured.

To what extent do you consider the value of the Estate damaged by the railway?
I do estimate the damage at a quarter part of the whole subject.

For many landowners, the building of the railways meant the destruction of farmland and the countryside profiting less from farming as a result. As the demands of the railway companies grew, Parliament forced them to seek permission to build further railways. This was not all plain sailing for them. Landowners began to look for settlement money before they agreed to their land being used. In 1846, Sir John Hall was party to an agreement with the North British Railway Company in which he agreed to give up all opposition to the Bill in Parliament called 'A Bill for making a Railway from the City of Edinburgh to the Town of Berwick upon Tweed with a Branch to Haddington'.

Source D

The said Sir John Hall shall convey to the North British Railway Company 50 acres of ground and works therewith connected including ground for building a station. The said company shall before breaking ground for the said railway or other works pay to the said Sir John Hall the sum of twelve thousand pounds sterling.

Part of an agreement between Sir John Hall and the North British Railway Company in 1846.

It was not just landowners who had reservations about the railways.

Source E

My stepmother took her place in the train. I can see her still, sitting in the carriage, as we children were taking leave of her. She had her handkerchief tightly pressed to her eyes so that she might see nothing and begged us not to make her uncover them. A more abject picture of terror and dejection I never saw. I remember well hearing the denunciations of the railroads: their dangers, their tendencies to injure health, their ruinous effect on trade, their causing cows to refuse to be milked, their ruin of the horse breeding trade, and many other imaginary calamities.

J. McDonald in his memoirs about an early train journey (1915).

> Study Sources B–E. Choose any source and explain the point of view it has and why this source is useful for conveying this point of view.

···❖ *Activity*

Working with a partner, discuss all the good and bad points of the railways. List them using evidence from the texts and any sources you can find. Each partner should then write a letter to the local paper expressing a different point of view. Remember to set out your letter to the editor with correct dates, and so on.

BUILDING THE RAILWAYS

The growth of the railways involved more than just laying railway tracks.

Many people with various areas of expertise were employed in building the railways. The tables below show the roles of some of them.

The Railway Company	
Owners and financiers	Builders
Shareholders	*Engineers*
Board of Directors	*Contractors*

Labour force	
Skilled workers	Unskilled workers
Brick layers	*Navvies*
Carpenters	*Runners*
Masons	*Excavators*

Building the railways was a fairly complex affair involving a lot of people and planning. The work was not easy and most of the railway companies had building problems.

Routes for trains provided the engineers with obstacles: trains had to encounter hills, sharp bends, rivers and all sorts of geographical challenges. Normally, a route would have to go round a hill, and if this was not possible, a tunnel had to be built. Bridges and viaducts also became part of the countryside, leading the railway over valleys and rivers. These were all built by the blood and sweat of the labourer or 'navvy' (short for navigator). The navvies travelled to where the lines were being built and so were constantly on the move. They took with them their own picks and shovels and hired themselves out to the railway companies. Their work involved hacking at the earth and rock with picks or shovels and often using gunpowder to tunnel into the earth.

Navvies' work was particularly dangerous – explosions and cave-ins were common. Their living conditions were terrible, consisting of small temporary huts that they often had to share with twelve other

Navvies constructing a railway (1884).

men. The huts had bunks and no furniture; cooking was on an open fire at one end of the hut. In some cases, the men paid a woman to cook for them but their diet was basic: bread, broth, barley, salt ham, herring and few vegetables. Scurvy was often a health problem for the navvy.

Source F

They made their home where they got their work. Some slept in huts constructed of damp turf, cut from wet grass, too low to stand upright.

A history of the English railway (J. Francis, 1851).

Source G

They have brought terror to our area. These filthy, horrible men curse and swear from dawn to dusk. At night they drink, spit and fight. No self-respecting person dares to leave their house after dark. This town will never be the same again.

A description of how people felt about navvies in their area in 1848.

Source H

For some years past, we have been in the habit of hearing of severe conflicts in different parts of Scotland with navvies and police. Men have been killed and valuable property destroyed …

The *Edinburgh Courant* in 1848.

Despite all this 'bad press' the navvies ensured that embankments were built, bridges constructed and the railway lines laid quickly. The work of the navvy was dangerous: many died or were injured in their everyday work life.

Source I

Accidents were common. Men were trapped between wagons, became buried under falls of earth, with limbs broken and bodies crushed.

A description by historian I. Olson (1944).

In the light of this, perhaps their lifestyle was understandable.

> Explain what the job of each of the following was:
>
> a) contractor   b) engineer.

···: Activity

Imagine you are working as a navvy and working on the railways. Write a letter to relatives in Ireland describing your work and a typical day for you. Set your letter out with proper dates and headings.

THE IMPACT OF THE RAILWAYS

By 1860, the railway network in Britain was nearly complete and by 1900 it served nearly every town in Britain. The advantages brought by the railways were huge – travel was more comfortable than by horse-drawn coach, fresh food could be delivered anywhere in the country and raw materials and goods could be delivered quickly.

Market people were soon loading railway trucks with goods on a daily basis – the effect of this was that people who would previously not have had access to market towns received a fresh supply of fruit, fish and vegetables. Farmers could also get animals to the market towns more easily and farm workers could travel to work. The fishing industry benefited with fresh fish being delivered inland. People from the countryside could now afford to travel into town to shop, so that more shops now opened.

The working classes could take holidays by the sea. This was made easier in the 1840s when new legislation stipulated that each new railway line was to provide at least one train a day in each direction and that the maximum fare to be charged for third class passengers was to be one penny per mile. Before now, rail travel had not been within the reach of the ordinary person.

Source J

The railways have given the lower classes great opportunities for leisure. Short trips give the working classes the chance to see places they would never have seen in the days of coaches and wagons. Factory workers can escape the dirt and bad air of the city and visit the countryside or the coast for short holidays. A railway train takes all classes of people from the wealthiest to the poorest in the land. Rich and poor come into contact with, and talk to, each other. Nothing is more educational than seeing new places and meeting new people.

Chamber's Journal, 1844.

Life changed for many Scots with the arrival of the railways. With railway lines reaching rural parts, tourism in Scotland flourished. In 1894, at a cost of £700,000, the West Coast line opened, running from Glasgow to Fort William and opening up the Scottish countryside for tourists.

Newspapers and mail reached people much quicker so that up-to-date information could be easily spread throughout the land. Time was standardised throughout Britain so that everyone now used Greenwich Mean Time.

By 1881 the railways had provided at least 18,000 more jobs. Jobs directly created included train drivers, station masters, railway guards and porters. In addition railways needed iron, steel and coal, creating more work in those industries. Around the central belt of Scotland in particular, workshops appeared to build and repair locomotives, carriages and wagons. In addition, locomotives and wagons could be sold abroad, to other countries which were also starting to build railways.

New towns developed around railway lines, specialising in this new industry. Existing towns changed in appearance as bridges, tunnels and stations were built. As the movement of goods for export became easier, ports and harbours grew.

However, canals and coach companies declined, as goods and raw materials could be moved more quickly by rail, and passengers were transported more quickly, cheaply and comfortably.

The impact of the railways on Scotland and the Scottish people was huge.

---

1   How did the railways help to make the town people healthier?

2   In what ways did cheap travel help poorer people?

⋯⋮ Activity

Using your notes and evidence from the chapter, explain fully the impact the railways had on life in the 1800s. Set this answer out with a clear introduction and conclusion. Give evidence to back up the points made in your answer.

Throughout the 1800s, the railways continued to develop. By this time, there was extensive use of machinery to cut and tunnel. Some natural obstacles, such as rivers, still caused problems. In 1890, a railway bridge was built crossing the River Forth in Edinburgh. The contract was awarded to Tancard, Arrol & Company on 21 December 1882. The total cost for the bridge was about £2.5 million plus £0.5 million for connecting railway lines. This was a huge financial investment for the time. During the construction of the bridge, 44 lives were lost, 93 injuries treated in hospital and 459 treated at home.

The Forth Rail Bridge under construction (1888).

The total length of the bridge is 5330ft (1624.6m); the whole length of the structure including both approach viaducts is 8295ft and 9.5in (2528.5m). The total allowance for expansion and contraction is between 6 and 7ft (1.8–2.1m).

The bridge was opened on 4 March 1890 by HRH the Prince of Wales and is still in use today.

Improvements and safety in rail travel	
Year	Change
1834	Introduction of signals and use of telegraph.
1881	Electric lighting on London to Brighton line.
1889	All coaches to have a brake fitted to stop coaches running away if they became detached from the engine.
1902	Electric signals and push button signalling. Boxes now controlled hundreds of miles of track.
1906	Dead Man's Handle fitted on every engine – an automatic stop on the train if the driver fell asleep or passed a stop signal.

By 1900, there was a fairly extensive network of railways throughout the country. Most railway companies were making huge profits and other industries benefited as a consequence – in particular the hospitality industry with hotels becoming an integral part of the landscape next to railway stations.

Until 1914, railways were the most popular form of public transport. Like the coal mines during the war, the railways were taken under state control. The government, however, wore out much of the rolling stock, coaches and engines. During the First World War, the demands put on the railways were great. Trains were used to transport troops and weapons, but with the demand to mobilise quickly came the development of other methods of transport.

By the 1920s, things were not going quite as well for the development of railways. The four new companies that were set up in 1921 to take the railways away from government control could not cope. The railways were also faced with competition from the roads. Lorries were being used to transport goods and buses now carried people to their work. Road transport was becoming more popular as well as cheaper. Cars were also beginning to contribute to the decline in the railway industry.

Edinburgh Waverley Station and the North British Hotel on Princes Street.

1 Show how technology helped to make travel by train much safer during this time.

2 Why was there a decline in the railways in the early twentieth century?

... IN CONCLUSION

···⟫ ■ There was a railway boom from the 1830s onwards.

■ The building of the railways needed the work of the navvies.

■ The railways opened up the country for many people and allowed people to commute to work.

■ New towns developed around railway lines and many jobs were created by the railways.

PRACTISE YOUR ENQUIRY SKILLS

Study the following sources carefully and answer the questions that follow. You should use your own knowledge where appropriate.

The issue for investigating is:

The development of the railways was to the benefit of ordinary people in Scotland.

Source K is from *Leaves from An Inspector's Logbook* by John Kerr (1915).

Source K

> The comforts, or rather discomforts, of railway travelling in the middle of the century were very different to those of the present day. Third class carriages were often little different from cattle trucks. For a considerable time they were open and had no seats. First and second class passengers were covered, and on the top the luggage of the passengers was packed, for there was no luggage van. There was no shelter for the guards (there were usually two), who, exposed to the weather, occupied seats on the top, one on the first and the other on the last carriage of the train.

Source L was written by historian R.N. Rundle in 1973.

Source L

> With the introduction of cheap workmen's fares, better paid workmen could live in a suburb and travel to work by train. The upper and middle classes moved further into the countryside, so villages near towns grew into towns. Holiday resorts were also created by the railway. Factories had no longer to be created on coalfields as coal could be carried cheaply by rail. However, coaching and canal systems were soon both badly affected.

1   How useful is Source K for investigating whether the railways did or did not benefit the ordinary people in the 1800s?

2   What evidence is there in Source K that the railways were not good for people travelling in the 1800s?

3   What evidence is there in Source L that the railways were good for people travelling in the 1800s?

4   How far do you agree that the railways were to the benefit of the ordinary people in the 1800s? Use evidence from the sources and your own knowledge to reach a conclusion.

ENQUIRY SKILLS: EXPLAINING THE ATTITUDE

These questions usually begin with words like:

1   Explain the attitude of the author towards …

In this type of answer you must use your own words otherwise the examiner will not know that you have understood the source and its interpretation fully. To start your answer you must make an overall comment on the attitude and only use short quotations as evidence. Clearly describe the attitudes conveyed in the source.

Question

1   Explain the attitude of the author in Source G on page 46 towards the navvies.

Answer

The author of Source G clearly does not have any sympathy for the Irish navvy working in Britain. He is of the opinion that they are frightening and violent men who have 'brought terror'. Not only are they violent, they are also constantly verbally abusive: they 'curse and swear from dawn to dusk.' The author views the behaviour of the navvy as so threatening that he maintains that people are scared to 'leave their house after dark'. His prediction is that the impact of the navvy is such that the town will suffer in the long term and not regain its peaceful status.

Comment

Here, the candidate states from the start the point of view they are going to take in the answer. The answer then goes on to use evidence from the source to substantiate the view and, while quotes are used, they are explained so that the answer is not merely a copy of the source in the question.

5 HOUSING AND HEALTH

How did housing affect public health?

What's it all about?

In this chapter you will learn about what the housing looked like, the problems of these houses, and the health problems involved. As a result of the changes brought about by the Industrial and Agrarian Revolutions, and the movement of the population, new industrial towns developed near the new industries. Housing was erected quickly and unplanned – this led to problems.

NEW TOWNS IN SCOTLAND

After 1760, new towns developed and expanded in Scotland – Glasgow, Greenock, Motherwell and Dundee, in particular, grew. These towns developed as a result of changes in agriculture and people being forced to find work in the new towns. By 1851, as many people lived in the towns as in the countryside. This huge influx to the towns completely changed the appearance of the towns and cities. The demand for housing was great with every spare room being rented out. In some areas, the wealthy abandoned the town centre and moved to better housing in the outskirts or suburbs. With this movement came many problems:

- overcrowding
- shoddily built houses
- irresponsible landlords
- bad sanitation
- lack of running water
- lack of windows and ventilation.

Source A

The problem of the housing of the working classes in London lives on through the centuries. It occupied the attention of our grandfathers … the problem arises in the first instance from overcrowding. Overcrowding is the multiplication of **manufactories** and workshops in larger centres … Generally speaking, the present condition of affairs is … due to two things – the increased birth rate and the migration of the rural population … In the train of overcrowding have come evils that threaten the health and the welfare not only of the overcrowded, but of the city itself.

George Sims, in *Living London*, 1902.

The problems facing London dwellers were nationwide – slums unfortunately became a feature of new industrial towns and presented society with many new problems.

> List in general terms the main problems of the new towns faced by the ordinary people living there.

Glossary

manufactories: factories.

Reasons for population growth in nineteenth century Glasgow.

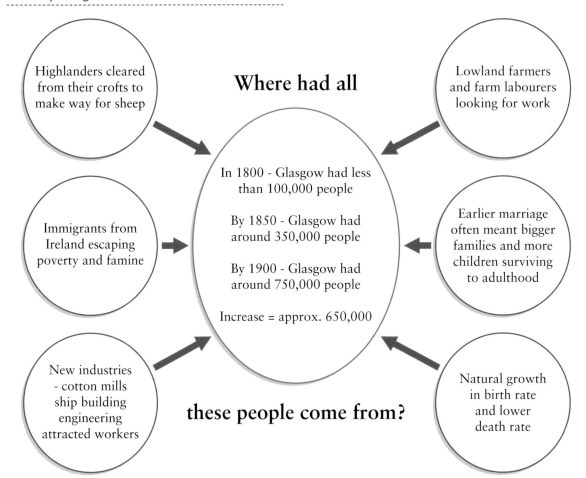

Highlanders cleared from their crofts to make way for sheep

Lowland farmers and farm labourers looking for work

Where had all

In 1800 - Glasgow had less than 100,000 people

By 1850 - Glasgow had around 350,000 people

By 1900 - Glasgow had around 750,000 people

Increase = approx. 650,000

Immigrants from Ireland escaping poverty and famine

Earlier marriage often meant bigger families and more children surviving to adulthood

New industries - cotton mills ship building engineering attracted workers

these people come from?

Natural growth in birth rate and lower death rate

The growth of towns and cities created huge pressure on, and demand for, housing.

HOUSING

In many of the towns, cheap housing was built quickly and without proper consideration to sanitation and services.

The need for housing led to rows of cheap houses that received no maintenance from landlords, whose only interest was in obtaining rent and not in meeting standards in their properties.

Tenement buildings in Glasgow.

In Scotland, tenement buildings were built since it was cheaper to build upwards rather than outwards as less land was used. Tenements were usually buildings of three or four stories with flats leading off the stairway.

Closes or wynds ran through the tenements providing access to a courtyard at the rear of the buildings where washing was dried, rubbish thrown and dry toilets situated. Most families lived in one room. These houses with one room became known in Glasgow as 'single ends'. The drawbacks of living in single ends are obvious – people had no privacy and if one family member caught an infection, there would be a high chance that other members would do so, too. Many of the single ends had no windows, allowing germs to breed rapidly.

Inside a Glasgow tenement. All the family lived in this one room.

Furniture in a single end was basic: beds were often in a recess with a curtain in an attempt to give a degree of privacy. Children often slept on the floor. Tables and chairs were luxury items for many. Water supplies had to be carried in from outside and there was no proper system of sanitation. Sometimes human waste was collected in what were known as cesspools – these were often adjacent to the water

supply! In Glasgow, the only water people drank was taken from the Clyde and people had to pay for it.

The government at the time was not interested in dealing with these problems as they followed a policy of *laissez-faire*; as a result, there were no laws to protect the tenants. Often they lived in accommodation that was tied to their job and so the loss of the job meant the loss of their home. From the 1830s on, there was a move away from this policy and changes were gradually introduced that would start to address the **social** problems of the time.

In Scotland in 1833, the Burgh Reform Act was introduced. Councils took money from the local rates to clean streets and to make sure, among other things, that slaughterhouses followed strict rules, a precaution that had an impact on the quality of food and diet. Over the years, this particular Act was added to and more improvements were made.

Glossary

social: to do with the people.

Source B

The great proportion of the dwellings of the poor are situated in very narrow and confined closes or alleys [which] have little ventilation, the spaces between the houses being so narrow as to exclude the action of the sun on the ground ... Greenock is the dirtiest town in the west of Scotland. It is often called 'Old Dirty'. There is a poor man living there with his wife and seven children in a dark room on the floor. The room is more fit for a coal cellar than a human being. It has one small window to give light. There is only one bed for the whole family but the rent for this room is half his income for the whole year.

Dr W.L. Lawrie reporting on conditions he saw in Greenock in 1842.

⋯⋅⋰ Activity

1 Measure out a space of fifteen feet by nine feet in your classroom and have fifteen people stand in it. Write a comment on the amount of free space there is.

2 Explain why there was so much poor housing in towns and cities in the nineteenth century.

3 Describe the problems many people faced in their homes in the nineteenth century.

Overcrowding was common with families living in these small and often damp houses, and although Dr Robert Grahams' description of Glasgow below is from 1818, it was accurate for much of the housing throughout the period of the 1800s.

Source C

We found in one lodging house, fifteen feet long, by nine feet from the front of the beds to the opposite wall, that fifteen people were sometimes accommodated.

Dr Robert Grahams, 1818.

Authors such as Charles Dickens have given us vivid descriptions of life in some of the slum areas.

Source D

Wretched houses with broken windows patched with rags and paper; every room let out to a different family, and in many instances to two or even three … filth everywhere – a gutter before the houses, and a drain behind – clothes drying, and slops emptying from the windows … men and women, in every variety of scanty and dirty apparel, lounging, scolding, drinking, smoking, squabbling, fighting and swearing …

Sketches by Boz by Charles Dickens, 1839.

Inside the houses the overcrowded conditions were appalling.

Source E

The dwellings of the poor are generally very filthy … those of the lowest grade often consist only of one small apartment, always ill-ventilated, both from the nature of its construction and from the densely peopled and confined locality in which it is situated. Many of them, besides, are damp and partly underground. A few of the lowest poor have a bedstead, but by far the larger portion have none; these make up a kind of bed on the floor with straw, on which a whole family are huddled together, some naked and the others in the same clothes they have worn during the day.

An Edinburgh doctor describing what he saw on his visits to homes in the 1840s.

These housing conditions led to inevitable health problems, which could be directly linked to the overcrowding and squalor that poor people found themselves in.

Trying to get landlords to make repairs was not easy. In 1902, George R. Sims quoted an interview he had with a woman in his book *Living London*.

Source F

I once interviewed a woman who, with her four children, was living in a wretched garret in a court in the Borough. It was a wet day, and the rain was coming through the broken roof and falling on a child who was lying on a bed in the corner. 'You should complain to the landlord,' I said, 'he is bound at least to give you a rainproof roof for your money.' 'Complain!' exclaimed the woman in a tone of horror; 'Yes, I should like to see myself doing it. I did complain to him once, when we were better off and lived in a room downstairs.

There was a brick loose in the wall and the rain had soaked through, and the plaster had given way till there was a hole as you could put your fist in – so I went to him, and said he ought to repair it.'

'And of course he did?'

'Yes, he did – he come and nailed the lid of a soap box across the hole, and he put the rent of the room up sixpence a week for improvement.'

George Sims, 1902.

Overcrowding and bad living conditions brought many other problems to the fore.

Source G

One of the saddest results of this overcrowding is the inevitable association of honest people with criminals. Often this is the family of an honest working man compelled to take refuge in a thieves' kitchen … Who can wonder that every evil flourishes in such hotbeds of vice and disease? … Ask if these men and women living together in these rookeries are married, and your simplicity will cause a smile. Nobody knows. Nobody cares … Incest is common; and no form of vice … attracts attention … The low parts of London are the sink into which the filthy and abominable from all parts of the country seem to flow.

W. C. Preston in *The Bitter Cry of Outcast London*, 1883.

··· Activity

In groups, discuss the problems associated with housing for the poor in cities. Use all your ideas produced during this discussion to produce a mind map. You can add as much information and as many illustrations as you want to this basic diagram:

Nineteenth-century housing for the poor

OTHER TOWN HOUSING

Not everyone lived in the slums in the cities. Better-off working-class families lived in houses with two rooms upstairs and two rooms downstairs. Middle-class housing ranged from large mansions to terraced houses with gardens, indoor toilets and piped water. Often they had rooms for servants. They did not live in the same part of the town as the working classes.

In the same way, the upper classes lived apart from the middle classes – they had large town houses as well as country dwellings. They also had large gardens, running water, baths and rooms for servants. Like the middle-class people, they were unaware of how bad housing was for some of the poorer people and so were unwilling to pay for the cost of better housing.

POST-FIRST WORLD WAR HOUSING

One of the first tasks taken on by the government after the First World War was to look at housing in the towns. Many of the men who had fought and died for their country had come from poorer areas. As the war had continued, politicians of the time had made promises of a better life after the war was over. Lloyd George, Prime Minister in November 1918 at the time peace was declared, promised this.

Source H

What is our task? To make Britain a fit country for heroes to live in. That is our first task. One of the ways of dealing with that is, of course, to deal with the housing conditions. Slums are not fit homes for the men who have won this war, or for their children.

They are not fit nurseries for the children and there must be no make do and mend. This problem has got to be undertaken in a way as never before, as a great national duty. It is too much to leave to the authorities alone. The housing of the people must be a national concern.

Lloyd George, 1918.

The Wheatley Act 1924 gave more money to councils to provide housing. More than 75,000 were built in Scotland; they all had electricity, indoor toilets and gardens. Housing schemes were built throughout the country, usually next to main roads leading out of towns.

By the 1920s, there was an improvement in housing.

Source I

The houses were built in pairs, or fours, all with gardens at the front and the back. The houses themselves varied in size from living room and two bedrooms, with bathroom and kitchen. The old slum houses were torn down and new houses built.

G. McAllister in his book *Houses that are Homes*, written in 1945, describes houses in Wishaw in Lanarkshire.

Improvements to housing	
Year	**Changes**
1833	**Scottish Municipal Reform** – this allowed rate payers to vote for local councillors and, as a result, some corrupt councils were replaced by those willing to improve towns.
1835	**The Municipal Corporation Act** – this allowed councils in England to improve lighting, sanitation and street paving – it still did nothing for slums.
1855	**Removal of Nuisances Act** – this allowed compulsory council purchase of slums.
1875	**Public Health Act** meant many houses had water and sewers.
1875	**Artisans' Dwelling Act** – councils were given the power to pull down slums and build new houses, but cost was a problem.
1909	**Housing and Town Planning Act** – local authorities could prepare town planning schemes.
1919	**Addison's Act** was passed to make 'Homes for Heroes' but funding ran out in 1921.
1924	**Wheatley Housing Act** – council houses were built with electricity, gardens and indoor toilets.
1930	**Green Woods Housing Act** – further large-scale clearance in slums.

···⊹ Activity

1 Describe in detail the living standards of the poor during the nineteenth century in the towns of Scotland.

2 In pairs, look at and discuss the laws that were introduced from 1855 to 1930. List the changes that these laws made, then add a list of improvements that you think were missing. Explain why you think further change was necessary. Present your thoughts in a manner that can be shared with others in the class. This can be done in the form of a talk, poster or PowerPoint presentation.

DISEASE IN TOWNS IN THE 1800S

The relationship between housing and health problems could be directly related. In 1842, Edwin Chadwick wrote in his 'Report on the **Sanitary** Conditions of the Labouring Population of Great Britain':

Source J

The annual loss of life from filth is greater than the loss from death or wounds in any wars in which the country has been involved in recent times. Disease is always found in connection with damp and filth and close and overcrowded dwellings.

Edwin Chadwick, 1842.

Glossary

sanitary: hygienic, clean.

midden: effluence deposits, sewage.

HOUSING AND DISEASE

Housing problems	Diseases caused
Poor sanitation – drainage cesspools, no running water	Cholera
Shared toilets	Cholera
Dirty stairs, and so on	Typhus, diphtheria
Open sewers and **middens**	Typhus
Rats and vermin	Typhus and typhoid
Poor diet	TB
Overcrowding	TB and typhus

The main killer of all of these diseases was cholera, with over 50 per cent of those who contracted it dying as a result. Between 1831 and 1832, over 10,000 people died of cholera in Scotland.

CASE STUDY: CHOLERA

In both the towns and countryside there was poor housing, but the people who lived in the towns were exposed to worse living conditions and more prevalent disease as there were so many families crowded together. Overcrowding and lack of drains caused the rapid spread of killer diseases such as smallpox, typhoid, tuberculosis (TB) and cholera. The 1800s saw a number of epidemics of cholera, one of the worst diseases. Symptoms included severe diarrhoea and dehydration, which led to shock and death in most cases.

Year	Deaths from cholera
1831	32,000
1848	62,000
1854	20,000
1866	14,000

The worst epidemics of cholera took place in the years 1831, 1848, 1854 and 1866, with both rich and poor dying as there was little escape from the disease. In the 1853/4 outbreak, of the 20,000 who died, it is interesting to note that over 6,000 lived in Glasgow. At first it was not realised that dirt, and in particular **contaminated** water, was connected to the disease, but by the 1840s, the government did start to take notice. In 1842, the 'Report on the Sanitary Conditions of the Labouring Population of Great Britain' recommended the following:

Source K

The most important things needed are drains, removing rubbish from streets, and purer water. There should be improved sewers and drains, and a medical officer of health should be put in charge of each district.

'Report on the Sanitary Conditions of the Labouring Population of Great Britain', 1842.

Glossary

contaminated: extremely dirty, spoiled, infected.

turncock: tap-like device for allowing water to flow from water well.

Source L was written by Dr John Snow in 1854 about the outbreak of cholera in London that year. He has clear ideas about the causes of it.

Source L

The most terrible outbreak of cholera has broken out in Broad Street. I suspect that the water in the much-used water pump in the street has been contaminated. In the last, large epidemic of 1848, almost 50,000 died from cholera.

Dr John Snow, 1854.

Source M

In the afternoon, those that pass that way … will find that there are from 25 to 30 people provided with bottles, pails, tubs, tea-kettles, broken jugs and other vessels … waiting for the **turncock** to make water flow from the main: and it is necessary to be in time, for many want to be supplied, and it runs only twenty minutes. At length, the water issues from a lead pipe of not more than half an inch in diameter, so small is the stream, that it is difficult, even for those who are provided with the proper vessels, to get what is wanted.

Another Blow for Life describes how water was collected in 1864.

Source N

'Monster Soup', cartoon published in 1830 about the state of London's drinking water, by George Cruikshank.

1 How important for people's health was a clean supply of water in the nineteenth century?

⋯⋗ Activity

Read over all the problems associated with water in the 1800s. In pairs, create a poster to illustrate the problems. Your poster should include:

- information on the contamination of the water

- how water was collected

- the effect of the problems with water on the lives of ordinary people.

The tenement building used as a cholera hospital in Dundee in 1826.

In the early 1800s, toilets were outdoors and shared by many families living in the same tenement block, and few public washing facilities were available for bathing. Usually, the poor used a privy – a shed containing a wooden seat under which was the cesspit. The cesspit was emptied by hand and the waste taken away at night in carts. The men who did this were known as muck majors!

A privy. This communal toilet was in the slums of Liverpool.

CHOLERA IN SCOTLAND

Dundee

Like other cities throughout Britain, Dundee and Glasgow fell victim to the outbreaks of cholera in the 1800s. In Dundee, a tenement building dating from 1744 was used as the cholera hospital for the city in 1826. The attraction of this building was its relative isolation from the rest of the city.

As with other cities at the time, Dundee in the nineteenth century was smelly and crowded, with noisy markets and narrow cobbled streets used by horses and carts and littered with deposits of horse dung. Street-side butchers and fish vendors, like those found at Butcher's Row and Fish Street, would often toss innards and unwanted flesh into street gutters. Householders threw refuse from tenement windows into the streets below.

Dung heaps were often situated too close to public wells and triggered complaints from citizens about their drinking water being contaminated with faeces. The city was in fact a cholera magnet.

> List all the factors that made Dundee a 'cholera magnet'.

Glasgow

In Glasgow, the problem was just as acute as in Dundee. Within the small area of the Gallowgate, High Street and Saltmarket, more than 20,000 people were crammed into sub-human housing. Overcrowding was only one part of the problem; dirt bred disease and while Glasgow was no stranger to typhus and typhoid, they were not ready for cholera.

The first bout of cholera in 1832 resulted in the deaths of 5100 people. The disease spread quickly and although it was Glasgow doctors who first caught on to the idea that dirt and disease were linked, it took until the later epidemics of 1848 and 1854 to focus attention more fully on this link.

Glasgow had been supplied, since the early part of the century, with water from the Clyde, but with the influence of the tide this water supply was often a mixture of water and the contents of the sewers. In 1847, the parish of Gorbals was given a supply of fresh water collected on the neighbouring hills.

Children playing in front of slum housing in Glasgow.

Source O

During the late cholera, there was a remarkable circumstance, which deserves notice as compared with the epidemic of 1839. Since the former period, the population of Glasgow, south of the Clyde, has nearly doubled; and with this exception, and the introduction of the soft-water supply, the circumstances might be considered as the same at both periods. In one district, the parish of Gorbals, the attack in 1832 was fearful; while Glasgow, north of the Clyde, also suffered severely. During the late epidemic (that of 1848–9), Gorbals parish furnished comparatively a small number of cases; while the epidemic in other parts of Glasgow was very severe. The unanimous opinion of the Medical Society was that this comparative immunity was to be attributed to the soft-water supply. I was informed that when the cholera was prevalent in Glasgow last winter, the parish of Gorbals again enjoyed a similar immunity from the disease.

Dr Leech, Glasgow (1850s).

This evidence helped the case of those who were aware of the link between water, dirt and disease.

When, in 1855, the registration of births, deaths and marriages was made compulsory, people had to declare the cause of death. It was at this point that James Russell used the new registration information to persuade the councillors and rate payers to fund an engineering scheme to transport water from Loch

Katrine into the city. This new water supply system was opened by Queen Victoria in 1859 and hailed at the time as a feat of engineering. It meant that Glaswegians no longer had to rely on the 30 public wells in the city or pay for water from some of the private suppliers.

Members of the Corporation Water Works Office's Water Committee on an inspection tour of the Loch Katrine Reservoir, 1876

A new sewage system of almost 50 miles was also put in place in the years between 1850 and 1875. These two improvements helped ease health and sanitation problems in the city. This forward thinking was soon taken further with refuse collection being organised, street lighting provided, and parks opened in the city – all in an attempt to improve the environment of the city. Much of this was done by local government and via the City Improvement Acts of 1860, when a large number of slums in the city were cleared.

1 Draw out a timeline of cholera and public health improvements made in Glasgow in the 1800s.

2 Explain why epidemic diseases were so common in Scottish cities in the nineteenth century.

Activity

Working in pairs, write a newspaper report on the opening of the Loch Katrine Water Scheme in 1859. In your report it would be useful to compare water supplies to the city before 1859 and evaluate the importance of this new scheme.

PUBLIC HEALTH NATIONALLY

Men such as Edwin Chadwick fought to get the government to take action nationally on public health. It was not until the first great cholera epidemic of 1831–2 that a series of reports were compiled into the state of towns in Britain. By far the most important of these was written in 1842 by Edwin Chadwick. Chadwick was born in Manchester and became a civil servant. In 1838, after reading a report into the industrial towns, he decided to carry out his own research. In 1842, he published his 'Report on the Sanitary Conditions of the Labouring Population of Great Britain'. This proved that life expectancy was much lower in towns than in the countryside.

Chadwick argued that it was possible for the government to improve people's lives by bringing about reform. He was not a 'do-gooder', as some people thought; he believed that a healthier population would be able to work harder and would cost less to support. He campaigned fervently for better sewerage systems and improved housing. His work was noticed, and with the realisation that cholera and a contaminated water supply correlated, the government set about bringing in public health laws.

Public Health Act 1848

- A board to set up local health boards was established.
- A central board was set up to make recommendations to the local boards.

Unfortunately, this Act was not successful as the boards had no real power and there were too few local boards set up. As a result, in 1858, it was abolished. However, in 1875, there was an attempt to bring more change.

Public Health Act 1875

- Local authorities had to appoint a Medical Officer.
- Authorities had to:
    cover and maintain sewers properly
    provide clean water
    pave and clean the streets.
- Local officers were appointed to check up on slaughterhouses and take responsibility to make sure that contaminated food was properly destroyed.

There were other factors that improved health.

- Better diet – due to better transport, fresh food reached the cities.
- Cheap new materials – soap and disinfectant reduced infections.
- Cheap cotton clothes – these were easy to clean and launder.
- Better medicines and hospitals.

Medical knowledge and developments were crucial.

Year	Discovery
1847	James Young Simpson discovered chloroform and its uses.
1864	Louis Pasteur discovered germs and microbes in relation to disease.
1867	Joseph Lister used antiseptics in surgery.
1882	Robert Koch discovered the germs that caused TB and cholera.
1895	X-rays were invented by William Roentgen.
1906	Calmette and Guerlin worked on a cure for TB.
1928	Alexander Fleming discovered penicillin.

⋯⋗ *Activity*

1 Working in pairs, copy the table from page 63 into your notes. Add another column and write the effects these changes to medicine would have on people.

2 Choose one of the improvements and, using the Internet and library, find out more about the improvement.

... IN CONCLUSION

⋯⋗ ■ The changes in industry and agriculture meant poor housing and growth of slum areas in most cities.

■ Houses were badly overcrowded inside and too closely built together.

■ There were problems with ventilation and sanitation.

■ Over time, there was a recognition of some of these problems and the government abandoned *laissez-faire* to bring in legislation.

■ By the turn of the twentieth century, most homes had indoor toilets and piped in water supplies.

■ Cholera, in particular, forced towns and cities to clean up their water supplies and take seriously the issues surrounding public health.

■ There were many other factors that led to improvements in health, for example, medicine and new discoveries at the time.

■ A rise in earning meant that people could afford better clothing and food.

PRACTISE YOUR ENQUIRY SKILLS

**Study the sources in this chapter carefully and answer the questions that follow.
You should use your own knowledge where appropriate.**

1 Look at Sources A–E on pages 51 and 53–4. Take each one in turn and explain why they provide us with useful evidence for investigating working-class housing in the 1800s.

2 Choose any two of these sources and explain why you think one is more valuable than the other. Use evidence from the sources and your own knowledge.

3 How useful is Source N on page 59 for giving information about water in the early nineteenth century?

4 Compare Sources K, L and N on pages 58–9 and explain where they agree or disagree.

5   The issue for investigating is:

Lack of hygiene was the main reason for the spread of disease in Scotland between 1830 and 1880.

Study the sources carefully and answer the questions which follow.
You should use your own knowledge where appropriate.

Source P is from a report written in 1842 on the Sanitary Conditions of the Labouring Population of Scotland. This extract describes conditions in Stirling.

Source P

> The filth of the prison floats down the public streets and gives off a disgusting smell. The slaughter house is near the top of the town, and the blood from it is allowed to flow down the public streets. There are no public toilets and the common stairs and closes, and even the public streets, are used as toilets.

Source Q is an account by Dr Arnott of conditions in Glasgow in 1842.

Source Q

> In Glasgow, the great mass of the fever cases occurred in the areas in which the poorest lived. In these dwellings we saw half dressed wretches crowding together to be warm. Although it was the middle of the day, several women were under a blanket, because other women were wearing the only set of clothes.
> Who can wonder that disease should spread in such situations!

Source R is from a report about conditions in Greenock in 1842.

Source R

> Most of the dwellings of the poor are in very narrow closes or alleys with little ventilation. The space between the houses is so narrow as to exclude the sun. The houses are generally two or three stories high, divided into flats with four or five families in each flat. They have one or two rooms each of about eight to ten feet square.

a)   How valuable is Source A for investigating the spread of disease in Scotland between 1830 and 1880?

b)   What evidence in the sources supports the view that lack of hygiene was the main reason for the spread of disease in Scotland between 1830 and 1880?

What evidence in the sources suggests that lack of hygiene was not the main reason for the spread of disease in Scotland between 1830 and 1880?

c)   How important do you think lack of hygiene was as a cause of the spread of disease in Scotland between 1830 and 1880? You should use evidence from the sources and your own knowledge to reach a balanced conclusion.
(SQA, 1999)

ANSWERING A KNOWLEDGE AND UNDERSTANDING QUESTION

Question

Source P is taken from *Life in One Room* written in 1885 by the Glasgow Medical Officer of Health.

Source P

> It is those single apartments that produce the high death rate of Glasgow. That high death rate shows an enormous proportion of deaths in childhood, and deaths from lung diseases at all ages. Of those who die in their first year, a third have never been seen in their sickness by any doctor. The bad air and the poor feeding fill our streets with bandy legged children suffering from rickets.

1   **Describe some of the health problems that were caused by the poverty in towns and cities in the nineteenth century.**

Answer

In the nineteenth century, there were many problems which were made worse by poverty. Housing problems and living in a single room meant that all the family were living in close quarters, sharing all the same facilities and often, as a result, disease. Many of the diseases were lung related, for example, tuberculosis, and affected both the young and the old. The young in particular were vulnerable as many, due to poverty and having to pay for medical help, had never been seen by a doctor. Ventilation problems and also poor diet meant that it was not uncommon for children to suffer from vitamin deficiency illnesses such as rickets.

Comments

Here the candidate gives a well-balanced response, combining recalled information with details extracted from the source. In all, there are four points from the source and four points from recall. Importantly, the candidate uses recalled information to expand upon and support what the source says, rather than just repeat it.

EXTENDED WRITING PRACTICE

Read over all the information you have about urban housing in the nineteenth century. To what extent did people's lives improve between 1830 and 1930 as a result of improvements in housing?

Present your answer in the form of an essay with a clear introduction and a conclusion that provides a balanced summary to the question of improved housing.

THE GROWTH OF DEMOCRACY

How did Britain become more democratic?

What's it all about?

Before the Reform Act 1832, many people in Britain had no say in the running of the country. There was no uniform system throughout the land that determined who had the right to vote, how people voted and who became MPs. Most of the **electoral** system was based on land and the wealth derived from it. By the 1800s, much of the wealth of the country came from industry. Industry was not represented in Parliament. The representative system was therefore not very democratic.

In your own words, describe the elements you would expect to see in a country that is seen as democratic. Mention who should vote, how they should vote, and so on.

CHANGES IN THE ELECTORAL SYSTEM

In Britain, the country was governed from London by the House of Commons, the House of Lords, and the monarch. Most Members of Parliament were landed gentry and represented the farming counties and therefore their own interests. The early years of the 1800s saw the Tory party in power in the Commons – they were made up largely of wealthy landed gentry and represented their own needs. However, by the mid-1850s, most of the people of Britain no longer lived in the countryside but in the ever-growing new towns of the Industrial Revolution, and their needs were very different from those of the people who lived in the countryside.

Glossary

democracy: a country ruled and governed by the majority of the people. Usually the government is freely elected by its people. From the Greek *demos* = people; *kratia* = rule.

electoral: relating to elections, involving voters.

	1801	1851	1901
London	957,000	2,362,000	4,536,000
Glasgow	77,000	329,000	776,000
Liverpool	82,000	376,000	704,000
Manchester	70,000	303,000	645,000
Birmingham	71,000	233,000	523,000
Sheffield	46,000	135,000	407,000
Cardiff	–	18,000	164,000

Population growth in the major cities.

The year 1832 was a crucial turning point in the process to remedy Britain's unrepresentative system.

Some changes	
Before 1832	**After 1832**
435,000 people had the right to vote	652,000 people could vote
An MP had to own land and was unpaid	MPs were still unpaid and had to own land
There was no secret voting	There was still no secret voting
Cities had no MPs	Some larger cities had two MPs

WHOM DID THE MPS REPRESENT?

Before 1832, the new large centres of population like Manchester, Glasgow or Birmingham had no MPs, while small villages with less then a dozen people were able to send two MPs to the House of Commons.

In the counties, the qualification for voting was to be a forty-shilling freeholder. In other words, to vote you had to have land that was worth more than forty shillings a year.

Voting took place on the hustings where voters publicly declared who they were voting for. The hustings was a wooden platform that was often in the town centre.

Source A

… a scene of struggling and pushing and fighting, succeeded to which we could do more justice than the mayor could, although he issued … orders to twelve constables to seize the ringleaders, who might amount in number to two hundred and fifty thereabouts.

Charles Dickens describing the hustings in his novel *The Pickwick Papers (1837)*.

To make changes in the way Parliament was voted in, and by whom, was a complex issue. Those already in power would be reluctant to alter the way Parliament was voted in, as this could take away their position of authority. Thus, it was very difficult to instigate any change. However, with all the changes brought about by changes in agriculture and industry, the demands on Parliament were different. The interests of farming and farmers were no longer the main concern of the people. The interests of many lay in industry and were represented by a new class of factory owners and workers. By 1832, the issue of parliamentary reform came to a head. There was a change in government and

Open voting at hustings before 1872.

the **Whigs** took over from the **Tories** after the latter had enjoyed a spell of almost 50 years in power. With the Whigs in power the gateway to parliamentary reform and to many other reforms was at last open.

From a practical point of view, what did all this mean? The electorate increased from 435,000 to 652,000 – not a great increase, still leaving five out of six men without the right to vote. In the **boroughs**, the middle class made an impact, but this was not the case in the counties where the landed gentry still ruled the roost. Some **radicals** did get into Parliament but certainly not enough to make an impact and bring about radical **social changes**. Perhaps the greatest significance of the Reform Act 1832 was that it led to a gradual programme of social reform and further parliamentary reform.

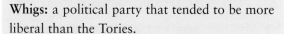

Towns now with two Members of Parliament

Towns now with one Member of Parliament

Counties gaining two extra Members of Parliament

Counties gaining one extra Member of Parliament

A map of England and Wales showing the increased parliamentary representation after 1832.

Glossary

Whigs: a political party that tended to be more liberal than the Tories.

Tories: earlier term for Conservative Party supporters. They supported the monarch and the Church of England.

boroughs: the same as Scottish burghs; in England, towns that had once been granted a royal charter.

radicals: people who wanted dramatic changes to Parliament and the way the country was run.

social changes: changes to the living and working conditions of the people.

POST-1832

Perhaps the greatest impact of the Reform Act 1832 was the fact that it led to further reforms, and between the years of 1832 and 1911 there was a series of parliamentary reforms.

1867 saw the next main event in parliamentary legislation and despite opposition to the bill, the Second Reform Act 1867 came into force.

Franchise qualification
In towns, the franchise was granted to: ■ male house owners over the age of 21 ■ male lodgers who paid £10 in rent per year. **In counties,** the franchise was given to: ■ males who owned property worth £5 per year ■ males who rented property of over £12 a year in England and Wales, and over £15 in Scotland.

Glossary

franchise: the right to vote.

In terms of the impact of the 1867 Act, there were over 1,200,000 new voters. Thirty-five boroughs lost one MP with seventeen losing two. Some counties gained MPs and many large cities were given a third MP. The 1867 Act in essence gave the vote to some of the urban working class. It also made a clear attempt to equalise the size of constituencies and seven more MPs were given to Scotland to represent the cities. In Glasgow alone, the electorate rose from 18,000 to 47,000. At the time, the Act was seen as a gamble and was referred to as a 'leap in the dark' as no one was sure how new voters would react.

THE SECRET BALLOT ACT 1872

Another crucial piece of legislation on the road to making Britain more democratic was the introduction of the Secret Ballot Act in 1872. This Act ensured that local landowners or employers could not put pressure on voters who perhaps depended on them for a home or living. Prior to the Act, voters could have found themselves victimised if they did not vote in a certain way.

Source B

Usually, an election day here has been a day of great political unrest and uproar. But today, the general aspect of things has changed. When the poll opened, the principal streets of the town were almost as quiet as usual.

At each polling booth there was erected the compartments as prescribed by the Act to secure the privacy of the voter while marking his ballot paper. These compartments consisted of an open, movable box with four stalls or recesses, each supplied with a small ledge to act as a desk, and placed back to back so that four voters might be engaged in marking their papers at one and the same time.

The Times newspaper, 14 September 1872.

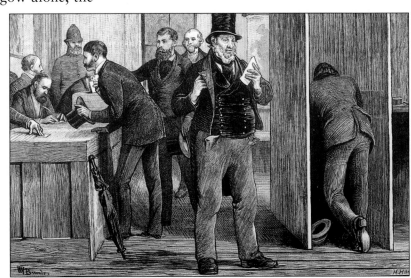

Voting by secret ballot after 1872.

IMPACT OF THE SECRET BALLOT ACT 1872

After 1872, elections were certainly a much more civilised affair with some control over the proceedings and people being allowed to vote as they wished.

Source C

Sir,

We are to have a ballot at last, after 40 years' struggle for it. The power of the Lords and the Commons has been too great. With the ballot, the voters will be able to return a different sort of man to the House of Commons.

But we must go on and get more. We must have a redistribution of seats. It will never do to let a town like Tamworth with 10,000 people return two MPs while Birmingham with 350,000 people only returns three. We shall not have honest laws until many landowners are replaced by working men: be they mechanics, traders, farmers or labourers, I do not mind who, so that they will make honest laws.

This letter appeared in *Reynolds' News*, 21 June 1872.

PAYMENT OF MPS

In 1911, MPs were given a salary for their work ensuring that for the first time working-class people could stand for Parliament. This helped the growth of the recently formed Labour Party, which looked specifically at the interests of the working classes. The life of Parliament was also to be limited to five years.

PARLIAMENTARY REFORM

Date	Reform	What it did
1867	Second Reform Act	Adult male householders in boroughs could now vote. Most middle-class people in towns and some of the workers gained the franchise.
1872	Secret Ballot Act	The secret ballot was introduced.
1883	Corrupt Practices Act	Candidates could only spend so much on their campaigns.
1884	Third Reform Act	Vote extended to males in the counties and some of the better-off workers could now vote.
1885	Redistribution of Seats Act	Constituencies were re-organised. Towns between 50,000 and 165,000 had two MPs. Scotland was given another 12 seats.
1911	Parliament Act	The power of the House of Lords was limited – they could no longer prevent bills becoming laws.
1911	Salaries for MPs	MPs were now paid a salary.

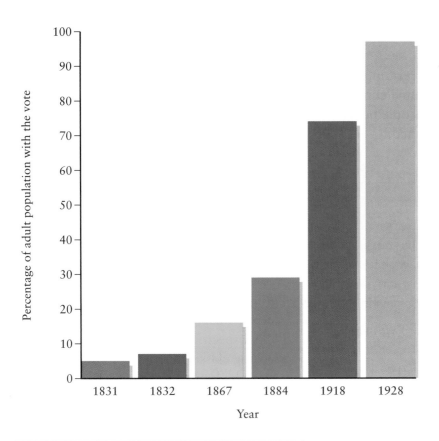

Increase in the electorate in Britain between 1831 and 1928.

⋯⟩ *Activity*

1   In what ways did each of these Acts make Britain more democratic?

2   In pairs, choose any one of the Acts on page 71 and carry out some research to find out as much as you can about it. Write up, and deliver, a short presentation explaining why you have chosen this Act and explain fully the impact you think it had on helping Britain become more democratic.

... IN CONCLUSION

⋯⟩   ▪ By the early 1800s, the parliamentary system was out of date.

   ▪ The new towns had no representation in the Commons, while sparsely populated places in the countryside still sent two MPs to the Commons.

   ▪ 1832 was a key year for introducing reform.

   ▪ 1867 took the 'leap in the dark' further.

   ▪ The years from 1832 up to 1911 saw a dramatic change in the franchise qualifications, voting conditions, and qualifications for MPs.

PRACTISE YOUR ENQUIRY SKILLS

**Study the sources in this chapter carefully and answer the questions that follow.
You should use your own knowledge where appropriate.**

1 Compare and describe the two forms of voting as described in Sources A and B on pages 68 and 70.

2 Is the writer of Source C on page 69 for or against the Secret Ballot Act? Provide evidence from the quote to back up your answer.

3 What other changes would the writer of Source C on page 71 still like to see take place and why?

Source D below is by modern historian Alastair Gray. In it he describes some of the changes in voting in Britain.

Source D

> In 1867, a Second Reform Act gave skilled workmen the vote and so 230,000 men in Scotland could take part in elections. In 1884, a Third Reform Act was passed. This meant that farm workers, crofters, miners and other working men could now vote.

4 How useful is this source in helping us find out about electoral changes in the late 1800s?

EXTENDED WRITING PRACTICE

Examine all the changes that had been introduced between 1832 and 1900. To what extent do you think Britain had become a democratic country by this point? In order to answer this question properly, list all the improvements that had been made, then all the changes that had not taken place. Take into account factors such as:

■ the number of people who could vote

■ the kind of people who could vote

■ the places that were represented in Parliament

■ how voting took place

■ the qualifications to become an MP.

Present your evidence in the form of an essay with a clear introduction and conclusion that provides a balanced answer to the question posed.

ANSWERING AN ENQUIRY SKILLS QUESTION

Question

1   How does the author in Source C on page 71 feel about the Secret Ballot Act 1872?

Answer

The author of the letter to the newspaper is very much in favour of the new legislation. He views the reform as a means to allow voters to vote how they wish to and without fear. He sees this Act as having a huge impact to the extent that 'a different sort of man' will be returned to the Commons. This Act for the writer is a start leading to even more parliamentary reform, with legislation for redistributing seats as his next goal. He wants 'honest laws' – laws that will meet the true needs of the people, that is, ordinary people who have not been truly represented by legislation up until this time.

Comments

The first two sentences clearly state how the candidate thinks the author feels about the Secret Ballot Act 1872. The candidate then uses quotes from the source to substantiate this view and is careful not just to repeat what the source says – the quotes are explained and evaluated to show how they support the candidate's answer.

7 WOMEN AND THE VOTE

How did women gain the vote in the twentieth century?

What's it all about?

This chapter explains why women wanted the vote, and why some people were opposed to votes for women. You will see the differences in the methods used by the **Suffragists** and the **Suffragettes** in their campaigns for the right to vote. The more militant tactics adopted by the Suffragettes gained huge publicity for the cause of women's suffrage, and pressure was also put on the government as a result of the part played by women on the Home Front during the First World War. After the war, the Representation of the People Acts were passed in 1918 and 1928.

In 2000, journalist Maureen Paton said, 'Of all the events that liberated women in the twentieth century, the greatest was enfranchisement [gaining the vote]. Winning the vote gave women a voice and an official stake in the community [that is, citizenship]. Emmeline Pankhurst is therefore indisputably the woman of the century'.

WHY DID WOMEN WANT THE VOTE?

Beyoncé Knowles demonstrates modern female success and independence.

In Britain recently, the Spice Girls sang about 'girl power', and today young women aspire to a career as well as a family life. Women have achieved success in employment and politics (Margaret Thatcher became the first woman Prime Minister in 1979), yet just over one hundred years ago women were treated as second-class citizens.

In the nineteenth century, women had very few rights. It was generally believed that women were inferior to men and they were denied equality in terms of education, employment and civil rights.

Source A illustrates the Victorian attitude to the education of girls.

Glossary

Suffragists: non-violent women supporters of the right to vote.

Suffragettes: violent women supporters of the right to vote.

Source A

The education of girls need not be of the same extended classical and commercial character as that of boys; they want more an education of the heart and feelings and especially of firm, fixed moral principles. The **profoundly** educated women rarely make good wives or mothers ... women who have stored their minds with Latin or Greek seldom have much knowledge of pies and puddings ... nor do they enjoy looking after children.

Sarah Sewell, 1868.

The Victorians believed that a woman's place was very much in the home.

Source B

The best they could hope for was marriage to a good man and a lifetime of keeping his house and **rearing** his children.

Historian Angela Holdsworth describes a view of nineteenth-century women.

Women could not legally own property and when a woman married, her belongings automatically became the property of her husband. In the second half of the nineteenth century, there were gradual improvements in the legal and educational position of women; however, they were still second-class citizens. Women could not participate in the political system: they did not have the right to vote in elections to Parliament, or to stand as a candidate. Many women saw the franchise as the key to women becoming citizens with equal rights to men. If women had the right to vote, then governments would have to pay more attention to the needs and interests of women.

Glossary

profoundly: deeply, well.

rearing: bringing up, as in children.

Source C

A poster of 1910 suggests that women should be allowed to vote.

1   How useful do you think Source A is as evidence of some of the problems facing women in the nineteenth century?

2   Write a paragraph to explain fully why women wanted the right to vote.

CAMPAIGNING FOR THE RIGHT TO VOTE

The Suffragists (NUWSS)

The National Union of Women's Suffrage Societies (NUWSS) was established in 1887 under the leadership of Millicent Fawcett. The Suffragists were mainly middle class and law abiding; in their campaign for the extension of the right to vote to women, the Suffragists believed in peaceful persuasion. The Suffragists wrote pamphlets and letters, held public meetings, sent petitions to the government and held peaceful demonstrations.

Source D

*The early Suffragists were a **well-connected** group of women who used their influence to try and persuade powerful men to take up their cause.*

Angela Holdworth describes the Suffragists in her book *Out of the Doll's House* (1988).

While many people assumed that the Suffragists were unsuccessful, they did establish a powerful organisation, which won the support of many politicians. By 1914, they had persuaded nearly half of the MPs to support votes for women.

The Suffragettes (WSPU)

Some women were critical of the Suffragist tactics, feeling that they had achieved nothing. Peaceful campaigning was not gaining them the vote. In 1903, Emmeline Pankhurst and her daughters, Christabel and Sylvia, established a new organisation, the Women's Social and Political Union (WSPU), whose motto was '**Deeds not Words**'. The Suffragettes were more **militant** and were determined to gain publicity for the cause of women's rights, even if that meant breaking the law.

The Suffragette campaign

The more militant tactics of the Suffragettes first came to public **prominence** in 1906 at an election meeting in Manchester. Two Suffragettes, Christabel Pankhurst and Annie Kenney, interrupted the Liberal politicians and asked: will the Liberals give women the vote? They were thrown out but continued to demonstrate outside. As a result, they were arrested and then sent to prison after refusing to pay a fine. These events made front page news in the popular press and the *Daily Mail* called the WSPU members 'Suffragettes'. The enormous publicity had three immediate results: men, and politicians in particular, began to take the Suffragettes more seriously; the Suffragettes realised that direct tactics could attract publicity for their cause; many young women joined the WSPU.

The value of the Suffragette campaign has led to much debate.

Glossary

well-connected: people who have influence with other important people.

'Deeds not Words': the motto of the Women's Social and Political Union (WSPU).

militant: favouring confrontational methods in support of a cause.

prominence: notice.

Source E

A suffragette demonstration to celebrate the release of two women prisoners from Holloway prison in 1908.

⋯⋗ Activity

Prepare a short speech to read out in class: either as a member of the WSPU supporting the Suffragettes, or as a male MP condemning their actions.

Source F

At one time, I thought it a great pity that the militant Suffragettes should create rows at Westminster. Now I have been brought round to another view. Nothing has done more for the cause of female suffrage than the militant Suffragettes. They have brought the question to the attention of the public and that is more than those who have carried on quietly for 60 years have achieved.

Part of a speech made by Dr Marion Gilchrist, a leading Suffragette. She was speaking in 1908 at the opening of the new WSPU headquarters in Glasgow.

Suffragette demonstrations became larger and more frequent, often **culminating** in clashes with the police.

Source G

The women were treated with the greatest brutality. They were pushed about in all directions and thrown down by the police. Their arms were twisted until they were almost broken. Their thumbs were forcibly bent back and they were tortured in other nameless ways that made one feel sick at the sight.

The Vice-President of the Royal College of Surgeons describes the treatment of Suffragette protesters in Downing Street (1909).

Glossary

culminating: resulting in.

Conciliation Bill: Bill of 1910 designed to reach a compromise between the government and the demands of the Suffragettes.

Attacks on property by the Suffragettes became common; windows were smashed with toffee hammers, famous paintings were slashed, telegraph wires were cut, post boxes were set on fire or attacked with acid (see **Source I**). Bowling greens and golf courses were also attacked with acid and there were even cases of arson.

In October 1909, the first militant demonstrations took place in Glasgow and Dundee. There seemed to be no end to the lengths that the women would go to in order to gain publicity. Whitekirk, a church in Edinburgh, was burned to the ground and campaigns continued despite arrests.

Suffragette militancy continued and escalated after the failure of the **Conciliation Bill**. Politicians, in particular, were targeted by the Suffragettes: they were heckled at meetings; prominent politicians, like Winston Churchill, were assaulted; Suffragettes chained themselves to the railings outside Downing Street; Emmeline Pankhurst and supporters tried to rush the House of Commons.

Source H

We are here, not because we are law-breakers; we are here in our effort to become law-makers.

Emmeline Pankhurst.

Source I

I was able to drop acid into the postal pillar boxes without being suspected, because I walked down from where I was employed in my cap, muslin apron and black frock … nobody would ever suspect me of dropping acid through the box.

The memories of a Scottish Suffragette, Jessie Stephenson in the 1920s.

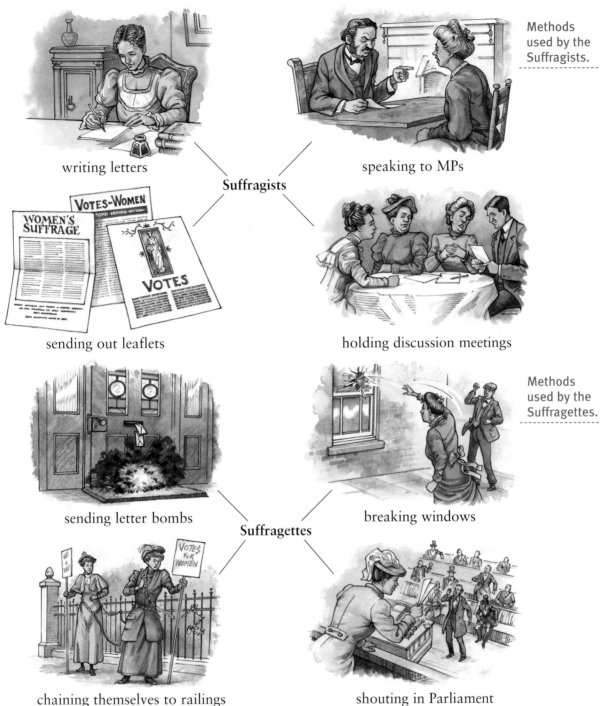

Methods used by the Suffragists.

writing letters

speaking to MPs

Suffragists

sending out leaflets

holding discussion meetings

Methods used by the Suffragettes.

sending letter bombs

breaking windows

Suffragettes

chaining themselves to railings

shouting in Parliament

The militant tactics of the Suffragettes led to the imprisonment of many women. However, even in prison they showed their determination in continuing to campaign by going on hunger strike. The first woman to go on hunger strike was a Scottish woman called Marion Wallace Dunlop, who was imprisoned in Holloway Prison in London. The government was alarmed as more and more Suffragettes followed her example and went on hunger strike. They were worried that a women would die, providing the Suffragette cause with a martyr. The government therefore introduced force feeding. In the medical report from Perth prison it was reported that Arabella Scott was held in isolation for 36 days and during that time attempts to force feed her were made three times a day.

Source J

The wardresses would enter with the apparatus: extricate and hold me in position, for example, flat on my back. Then the doctor greased the tube and inserted the gag. Then I would close my eyes and pray that I should have no feelings of resentment or anger towards those who caused me pain. I always dreaded the insertion of the tube, which was accompanied by dry retching and choking sensations ...

On removal of the gag my head was seized, my jaws and lips held tightly together. Sometimes ... the food would be returned into my mouth, and unable to escape would burst through my nose. Then my nose would be pinched, and I was ordered to swallow it again ... I was held in this way from one to two hours after each operation.

Arabella Scott describes her experience of being force fed in Perth Prison.

If the hunger strikes provided evidence of the determination of the Suffragettes to win the vote, the events of 4 June 1913 underlined just how serious they were. Emily Davison, a Suffragette, rushed on to the Epsom race course during the Derby. It is not certain whether she simply wanted to display the Suffragette colours and disrupt the race, thus gaining publicity for the cause ... or ... she intentionally threw herself under the king's horse, Anmer. Whatever her thinking, she was fatally injured and died a few days later. The Suffragettes now had a martyr and her funeral was attended by thousands.

> Write a paragraph to explain fully why women wanted the right to vote.

Source K

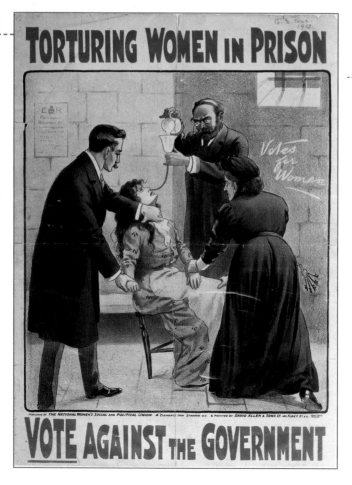

A WSPU poster from 1910 giving the Suffragette view of force feeding.

Emily Davison being struck by the king's horse, Anmer, at the Epsom Derby in June 1913.

Emily Davison's funeral procession passes through Piccadilly Circus, London on 14 June 1913.

A Suffragette poster of 1913 gives the WSPU reaction to the Temporary Discharge Act.

The brutality of force feeding led the government to review their treatment of imprisoned Suffragettes and in 1913 the Temporary Discharge Act was introduced (nicknamed the Cat and Mouse Act by the WSPU). This Act allowed protesting women to be released until they had regained their strength – at which point they would be re-arrested: very much like the game of trapping and releasing mice as performed by cats.

1   How did the women who were arrested deal with their imprisonment?

2   Explain the dilemma this gave to the government at the time and describe what they did to counter this quandary.

Opposition to the Votes for Women campaign

Source L

Because of the violent campaign of the Suffragettes … the cause of women's rights had marched backwards.

Winston Churchill comments on the militant campaign of the Suffragettes.

Source M

The time for dealing gently with the idle, mischievous women who call themselves militant Suffragettes has gone by.

A *Daily Express* leader writer in 1908 urging the government to take strong action against the Suffragettes.

The struggle for the vote continued in this way up until the outbreak of war in August 1914 with both peaceful and violent campaigning taking place.

Explain why some people were against the Votes for Women campaign.

⋯⟡ Activity

Using information from this chapter about the campaigning methods of the Suffragists and Suffragettes, copy and complete the table below, inserting rows as necessary.

Suffragist methods	Suffragette methods

WOMEN AND THE FIRST WORLD WAR

The struggle for the vote continued until August 1914 when the world was thrown into chaos when war broke out. Women turned their attention to the common enemy at this point and abandoned their campaign for the vote. Instead of the slogan 'the right to vote', they adopted the one of 'right to serve'. Women took up posts in all sorts of jobs in munitions factories to the extent that by 1917 over 800,000 women worked in the munitions industry. They became involved in the Land Army, taking the jobs the men who were fighting had been doing. They worked as drivers and bus conductors, in the police and on the railways.

Some women even went overseas and helped at the front, nursing and driving ambulances or working in intelligence. Their war effort was enormous and acknowledged by many.

Source N

The home front is always underrated by generals in the field. And yet that is where the Great War was won and lost.

Lloyd George.

Women working in a Manchester munitions factory in 1918.

WHY DID WOMEN GAIN THE VOTE?

This is an issue which has divided opinion from the time of the campaign to the present day, as can be seen from sources O to W.

Source O

Women have tried reason, argument and pleading without success. They are now convinced that they will not be treated as persons until they make themselves a nuisance and a terror.

They say if they cannot gain the vote using reason and argument, then force must be used.

And who are we to criticise them? Have you forgotten the Chartist times when men were engaged in militancy to gain the vote? Particular acts we may disapprove of, but surely we can admire the spirit, the fearlessness and the courage of the Woman Militant.

An extract from *Forward*, a newspaper that campaigned for women's suffrage, published on 1 March 1913.

Source P

If, instead of Mrs Pankhurst making such scenes in London, the Suffragettes were to follow the non-militant methods of the Women's Suffrage League, the vote would soon be won. If people had the opportunity of hearing the logical arguments of the Women's Suffrage League, and if Cabinet Ministers had that privilege, the vote would be won without delay. Let the WSPU take a leaf from the book of the Women's Suffrage League.

An extract from a letter by Mr John Hunter, published in the *Glasgow Herald* on 17 July 1913.

Source Q

The Suffragists always kept their efforts within the law while the Suffragettes were prepared to break the law.

A modern historian describes the differences between Suffragist and Suffragette tactics.

Source R

Despite the opposition from politicians, the press and the public, the organisation for women's suffrage seemed to be prospering. By 1909, the WSPU had branches all over the country, 75 paid office staff, and a newspaper, *Votes for Women*, which sold over 20,000 copies per week and was read by many more.

A modern historian describes the Suffragette organisation.

Source S

By the early twentieth century, the peaceful persuasion of the Suffragists had convinced many men that women should have the vote, but women were still denied the vote. Nothing raised awareness of the cause of votes for women more than the militancy of the Suffragettes. However, many people of both sexes felt that these lawless Suffragettes were an obstacle to women's suffrage.

A modern historian comments on reasons why women gained the vote in 1918.

Source T

The war increased the social and economic importance of women as they filled in for the shortage of men. Above all, in their awareness that they were performing arduous and worthwhile tasks and living through experiences once confined to only the most adventurous of men, they gained a new self-consciousness and a new sense of status.

Marwick, a historian, describes the effect of the First World War on women.

Source U

Women proved by their work in the First World War that they deserved the vote equally with men. Thus their war efforts succeeded where the Suffragette campaign had failed.

Historian John Ray.

Source V

Women were campaigning for equal rights from the 1850s and the First World War was the culmination of that campaign, not in itself the cause of female emancipation.

Adapted from a modern historian.

Source W

War smoothed the way for democracy – it is one of the few things to be said in its favour.

Historian A.J.P. Taylor.

REPRESENTATION OF THE PEOPLE ACTS

Representation of the People Act 1918

- Women over the age of 30 who were householders gained the franchise.

Representation of the People Act 1928

- Women over 21 got the vote.

- Women were now on an equal footing with men.

Getting the vote helped liberate women. However, the war also had an important effect on women's increasing freedom. During the war, women had taken on new roles, but many were expected to return to their former ways after the war. For those who were allowed to keep their war-time jobs, new issues arose such as the question of pay; it was going to be a long struggle before women were entitled to receive the same pay as a man for carrying out the same job. However, perhaps the most important outcome for women was that attitudes were starting to change. Women had become more confident and men had begun to realise that women deserved to be treated as equals. Women had more freedom and they celebrated this by wearing short dresses, trousers, and short hairstyles.

In 1919, women were allowed to enter professions such as law or architecture, and in 1921 contraception became available for women for the first time. Women now had much more control over their lives.

'New women' in 1925.

> **⋯⋮ Activity**
>
> In pairs, design a poster to recruit women to work during the war. Include as many types of work as you can. You can use some of the examples from the sources or ones of your own that you have found on the Internet or in the school library.

... In Conclusion

···▷ ■ The NUWSS or Suffragists used peaceful methods to try to gain the vote.

■ The WSPU or Suffragettes used violent methods to try to gain the vote.

■ The consequences of the actions of the WSPU led to imprisonment, hunger strikes and the 'Cat and Mouse' Act 1913.

■ Women had very little say in the running of the country in the late 1800s.

■ Women looked on the vote and a say in Parliament as the way to improve their living and working conditions.

■ During the war years, women focused on the war effort and kept the home front going, making a huge contribution to winning the war.

■ In 1918 and 1928, women were given the right to vote.

■ The war effort had an impact on many other aspects of women's lives, for example, fashion and status.

PRACTISE YOUR ENQUIRY SKILLS

Study the sources in this chapter carefully and answer the questions that follow. You should use your own knowledge where appropriate.

1   Explain the point of view being expressed in Source H on page 78.

2   How reliable is Source K on page 80 as evidence of force feeding?

3   Look at Sources J and K on page 80. To what extent do Sources J and K agree about how female prisoners were treated?

4   The issue for investigating is:

The actions of Suffragettes harmed the cause of votes for women.

Source X is an extract from *Women's Suffrage* by Millicent Fawcett, a founder of the Suffragists, in 1912.

Source X

> The Women's Social and Political Union had not attracted any public notice until 1905. By adopting new and startling methods, they succeeded in drawing a large amount of public attention to the cause of votes for women. However, many campaigners viewed these methods with disgust. They believed that lawful, peaceful action would prove more effective in the long run as a way of converting the public and the government to believe in women's suffrage.

a) How useful is Source X for investigating the effect of the Suffragette campaign?

b) What evidence is there in Source X that agrees that Suffragettes harmed the cause of votes for women?

c) What evidence is there in Source X that shows that the Suffragettes did not harm the cause of votes for women?

d) How true is it to say that the actions of the Suffragettes harmed the cause of votes for women?

Use all the evidence from the sources and your own knowledge to reach a balanced conclusion.

ANSWERING AN ENQUIRY SKILLS QUESTION

Question

Source C on page 76 is a poster published in 1910.

1 How useful is Source C as evidence of some of the problems facing women at the turn of the century?

Answer

Source C is a poster from a period in time when the women were campaigning for an improvement in their status. This primary source is one provided by women who were campaigning for the right to vote, so it is possible that it is exaggerating their position. However, it was a fact that women did not have the right to vote, in the same way as convicts and inhabitants of mental institutions, as illustrated accurately in the poster. The purpose of the poster is clearly to highlight the plight of women in the early twentieth century.

Comments

Here the candidate works through the details of the source, such as who it was written and drawn by, to what period it belongs, and what message it is trying to get across. The candidate then uses some of their own knowledge to demonstrate what the purpose of the source is and what it is trying to achieve.

EXTENDED WRITING PRACTICE

Read over all the information you have about women in the early 1900s. How important were the Suffragettes in the campaign to win votes for women? In order to answer this question properly, examine the campaigns of both the Suffragists and Suffragettes as well as the role played by women during the conflict of 1914–18.

Present your answer in the form of an essay with a clear introduction and a summary that provides a balanced conclusion to that question.

SUMMARY

Change in the hundred years between 1830 and 1930

The study of this unit is part of the Standard Grade course appropriately called 'Changing Life in Scotland and Britain'. This period in time between the 1830s and 1930s saw great change for every person in every country. Homes, work, buildings, health, jobs and society changed dramatically. It was also a time of invention – new transport and technology were developed, having a huge impact on the everyday lives of ordinary people in both the towns and the countryside.

POPULATION CHANGES

The trigger for all this change centred on the rising and mobile population, which led to changes in working habits and ideas. Better diet and health provision ensured that people were living longer and more children were surviving into adulthood. Better diet came about as a result of changes in agriculture and the production of food. However, these changes in agriculture, and the technology of agriculture, made many people surplus to requirements and thus unemployed. At around the same time, the abandonment of the domestic system for factory work occurred, paving the way for the development of town life.

INDUSTRIAL CHANGES

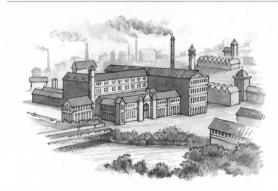

New town life expanded greatly around industry and brought people together in much larger numbers than ever before. All classes of people now lived in the towns within close proximity to the factories which they either worked in or owned. A new class of industrial people also emerged at the level of entrepreneurs and skilled workers. These people formed what became known as the middle classes. They had different needs from workers in other areas of life and pressed for change to the outdated parliamentary system through the emerging trade unions. Towards the end of this period, women were also exercising their rights to have a say in their lives and future.

AGRICULTURAL CHANGES

In the countryside, the Highlands of Scotland and in Ireland, nature and changes in agriculture played a role in bringing about change. Potato blight as well as new profitable approaches to farming caused a mass exodus to the towns of Britain and overseas.

IMPACT

Communication

People could now meet and communicate more readily, sharing ideas and using the new transport system set up by the railway network. The development of the railway industry also meant that newspapers and post could reach all parts of the country and so everyone was aware of the latest news and developments. Politicians could ensure that their views were heard, not only in the cities but also in the smaller towns throughout the land.

THE TURNING POINT

Power was now steam based and the role of the coal mines in industry was crucial up until the First World War.

The 1914–18 war was a turning point for many of the changes of this period and had a huge impact on many of the changes that had been taking place. For example, women in this period abandoned their struggle for the vote to face the common enemy of Germany. Industrial strife was also halted as men enlisted for the war. Motor transport and developments in technology had a long-term impact on the coal and rail industries, with road transport and electricity taking over much of what had previously been done by rail or coal.

···: Activity

In groups, choose one of the following areas of development.

Population Changes

Industrial Changes

Agricultural Changes

Follow your chosen topic throughout this period of change. Look at why the changes occurred, what the changes were and the impact of the changes. To do this you must show that you have made use of a variety of resources – these can be your notes, primary or secondary sources, books and the Internet.

Prepare your work to show others. This can either take the form of a talk, PowerPoint demonstration or wall display so that your findings can be shared with the rest of the class. Your talk/display must conclude with a clear explanation of the impact of the changes you have looked at.

INDEX

S 999 HIS A

Heinemann Scottish History for Standard Grade

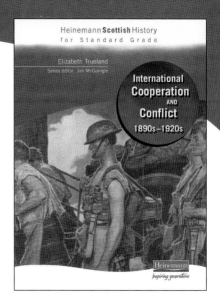

Heinemann **Scottish** History
for Standard Grade

Elizabeth Trueland
Series editor: Jim McGonigle

International Cooperation AND Conflict 1890s–1920s

Endorsed by SATH as the most up-to-date texts for Standard Grade!

These books provide everything needed to prepare students for their exams in the four most popular topic areas: *Changing Life in Scotland and Britain 1830s-1930s, International Cooperation and Conflict 1890s-1920s, Russia 1914-41* and *Germany 1918-39*.

◆ Written by experienced History PTs to cover the most recent Standard Grade requirements.

◆ Plenty of exam-style questions help students prepare for the exam.

◆ The attractive full-colour presentation motivates students to perform their very best.

Heinemann **Scottish** History
for Standard Grade

John Kerr
Series editor: Jim McGonigle

Germany 1918–39

Germany 1918-39
0 435 32693 7

International Cooperation and Conflict 1890s-1920s
0 435 32690 2

Changing Life in Scotland and Britain 1830s-1930s
0 435 32692 9

Russia 1914-41
0 435 32691 0

 01865 888068  01865 314029  orders@heinemann.co.uk  www.heinemann.co.uk

Heinemann
Inspiring generations

H176 R

S 999 HIS A

Heinemann Scottish History

Endorsed by SATH for S1 and S2

- Each book is endorsed by SATH for S1 and S2 and SATH members are eligible for a discount – contact us for more details!

- Each of the five Pupil Books covers one of the key aspects of study recommended in the 5-14 Guidelines, to ensure your pupils cover the required content.

- A wealth of skills questions help you to develop and monitor your pupils' understanding and thinking processes, and encourage them to explore the subject for themselves.

- Outline studies introduce topics to your pupils while in-depth investigations provide the motivating, detailed historical knowledge that they will need.

The Ancient World
0 435 32091 2

The Kingdom of Scotland in the Middle Ages 400-1450
0 435 32094 7

The Twentieth Century
0 435 32093 9

Renaissance, Reformation and the Age of Discovery 1450-1700
0 435 32090 4

The Age of Revolutions 1700-1900
0 435 32092 0

Simply contact our Customer Services Department for more details:

(t) 01865 888068   (f) 01865 314029   (e) orders@heinemann.co.uk   (w) www.heinemann.co.uk

Heinemann
Inspiring generations